The Impact of Natural Disasters on Systemic Political and Social Inequities in the U.S.

The Impact of Natural Disasters on Systemic Political and Social Inequities in the U.S.

Edited by
Paul S. Adams and Geoffrey L. Wood

LEXINGTON BOOKS
Lanham • Boulder • New York • London

Published by Lexington Books
An imprint of The Rowman & Littlefield Publishing Group, Inc.
4501 Forbes Boulevard, Suite 200, Lanham, Maryland 20706
www.rowman.com

6 Tinworth Street, London SE11 5AL, United Kingdom

British Library Cataloguing in Publication Information Available

Library of Congress Cataloging-in-Publication Data

Names: Adams, Paul S., editor. | Wood, Geoffrey L., 1970– editor.
Title: The impact of natural disasters on systemic political and social
    inequities in the U.S. / edted by Paul S. Adams and Geoffrey L. Wood.
Description: Lanham : Lexington Books, [2021] | Includes bibliographical
    references and index. | Summary: "The Impact of Natural Disasters on
    Systemic Political and Social Inequities in the U.S. examines how
    natural disasters impact social inequality in the United States. The
    contributors study social and political mechanisms in disaster response
    and relief that enable natural disasters to worsen inequalities in
    America"— Provided by publisher.
Identifiers: LCCN 2020039707 (print) | LCCN 2020039708 (ebook) | ISBN
    9781793627995 (cloth ; alk. paper) | ISBN 9781793628008 (ebook)
Subjects: LCSH: Disaster relief—Political aspects—United States. |
    Emergency management—Political aspects—United States. | Disaster
    victims—United States—Social conditions. | Discrimination—United
    States. | Marginality, Social—United States. | Social
    stratification—United States. | Equality—United States.
Classification: LCC HV555.U6 I56 2021 (print) | LCC HV555.U6 (ebook) |
    DDC 363.34/40973—dc23
LC record available at https://lccn.loc.gov/2020039707
LC ebook record available at https://lccn.loc.gov/2020039708

Contents

Acknowledgments

PAUL S. ADAMS

I would like to thank three of my most influential professors from the University of Massachusetts-Amherst who all passed away in the past few years. Dr. Howard J. Wiarda, who passed away in 2015, was a mentor in so many ways and recruited me to Comparative Politics through his interest in me as a graduate student and nascent scholar. Dr. Jerry Mileur, who passed away in 2017, was generous and kind, despite being a St. Louis Cardinals fan, and always willing to provide good advice. Dr. George Sulzner, who passed in 2018, was generous with his time and his good spirit. I had many great role models during my UMass years; Howard, Jerry, and George are missed.

GEOFFREY L. WOOD

I would like to thank my wife, Cindy, and my son Trenton for always supporting me. I dedicate this volume to Loretta, Neva, and Pamela. They began the journey with me and continue to inspire me even today.

Chapter 1

The Impact of Natural Disasters on Inequities

Exploring New Paradigms and Relevant Evidence

Geoffrey L. Wood

The impact of natural disasters in the United States on increasing political marginalization and social inequality is both understudied and misunderstood. Some of the reason for this is the absence of a theoretical and methodological paradigm, which could better provide explanatory power in discovering how natural disasters impact political and social inequities. Such a paradigm could then lead to the development of scholarship through the application of theories and methods to examine how natural disasters affect the people who have lived through them. Over the last twenty years, there have been several natural disasters which have impacted the United States. While these events have led to billions of dollars in property damage and the loss of countless human lives, the responses to these disasters at the federal, state, local, and neighborhood levels have been uneven.

The purpose of this introductory chapter is twofold. First, we will discuss previous work examining theoretical constructs, notably historical categorical inequality and critical demography, and the ways in which these are applicable to the study of natural disasters. In earlier work, Geoff Wood examined how Hurricane Katrina devasted New Orleans in 2005. Rather than relying on traditional individualistic status attainment models or conventional demography measures, Wood took a different approach to include institutional, systemic, and structural factors in order to show how people were affected on the basis of their position in society (Wood 2016). The first part of this chapter will be a review and reintegration of these theoretical constructs and their application to natural disasters. The second part of the chapter will introduce the work of the scholars who have contributed to this edited volume. Although each of these contributions come from differing theoretical and methodological angles, the focus remains on looking at how political and social inequities are shaped by a natural disaster event. Some contributions examine the topic from a theoretical and comprehensive perspective, while others are case studies. However, each piece offers another viewpoint in exploring the ways in which natural disasters affect and shape peoples' social, economic, and political lives.

For the past fifty years, conventional demography has been at the heart of much work done in the social sciences. We argue that while conventional demography provides details on the population characteristics of people living in an area, it does a poor job of explaining the how and why of those characteristics. One of the first moves away from conventional demography began in the late 1990s, with a move to a paradigm which provides better explanations for how and why events occur.

CRITICAL DEMOGRAPHY

In earlier work, Horton (1999) outlined the distinctions between conventional and critical demography, and then argued that critical demography was more important in discovering nuanced historical processes affecting people. While conventional demography has relied on static variables, trends, and estimates of changes in population parameters, critical demography is explanatory, predictive, and explores dimensions of power and social structure. Although events are not packaged for quantitative analyses as conventional demographers would prefer, contextual and relational nuances remain important for structural explanations of how and why. Also, conventional demography relies on assumptions of the ways in which society should work, but critical demography examines issues of social structure differentiation and power (Wood 2017). In the case of examining natural disasters, this is an important distinction.

Critical demography can further be extended as an explanatory paradigm when examining the impact of natural disasters on differing population groups. It is careless and short sighted to evaluate natural disasters through a lens where power is excluded as a factor. Social differentiation and power have set the stage in our communities since the founding of this country, and these pieces are critical for both diagnosing and solving problems that occur in communities as a result of a natural disaster (Wood 2017).

America has a well-known history of residential segregation by race and class. Conventional demography will count the people living in neighborhoods with respect to their race, gender, class, or age; however, this tells little of the power or social differentiations of these people. A critical demography lens allows exploration of these high levels of neighborhood or residential segregation, which are often in place before a natural disaster occurs. Property values vary a great deal by neighborhood in that homes located in the suburbs, typically occupied by whiter, wealthier families, tend to have higher property values than those located in inner-city neighborhoods, occupied by poorer, minority families (Wood 2018). Income and wealth differences in richer suburbs versus poorer urban neighborhoods have an amazing effect on the response from organizations and governmental entities after a natural disaster. Often, these differences in resources can also account for natural disaster preparedness as well.

Horton (1999) has argued convincingly that we cannot understand the concept of race without understanding the role of racism, and this is as true for residential segregation by race when examining communities impacted by natural disasters. This logic also extends to other demographic variables as well. We cannot look at race, class, or gender without also examining racism, classism, and sexism, which are inherent to how these categories were established in the first place. For example, as race cannot be properly understood without examining the power of racism in historical socioeconomic perspective, racially segregated neighborhoods cannot be addressed without first uncovering the history of racism, its impact on the social structure, and the resulting different levels of power that social structure differentiation produces in American society (Wood 2017, 2018).

In terms of critical demography, we argue this paradigm provides better tools to examine demographic characteristics of people than does conventional demography. Specifically, in the case of natural disasters, critical demography allows us to better measure the role of historical circumstances and power differentiations, which are present in demographic categories. Rather than simply counting and describing the population, critical demography allows us to question the status quo and assumptions built into a system on the basis of power by digging deeper into questions of how and why demographic categories matter. Similar to critical demography as a methodological tool of importance, Charles Tilly's development of historical categorical inequality has shown great promise as a theoretical paradigm capable of providing much explanation when exploring natural disasters.

HISTORICAL CATEGORICAL INEQUALITY

When considering the impact of natural disasters on political and social inequities, Tilly (1998) explored the ways in which individual patterns were set, and then incorporated these patterns into institutional processes. He argued paired unequal categories set inequality in place and this inequality

allowed organizations and institutions to use these patterned sets for decision making. Much like conventional demography discussed earlier, status
attainment research focused on individuals, and tended to ignore contextual, social structure, and power relations (Tilly 1998). Tilly argued against
status attainment models, as Horton (1999) argued against conventional
demography, for similar reasons. The role of paired unequal categories to
set categorical inequality is congruent with examining the ways in which
power and social structure shape outcomes in critical demography (Wood
2019).

In the case of natural disasters, these categories of inequality formed over
time and were then used to determine how resources would be allocated. In
fact, natural disasters often act as an accelerant of inequality. During times of
crisis, these categories are easy to rely upon as resource allocation decisions
are made. Tilly stressed such categories resulted in an unequal distribution
of rewards and privileges from the moment the categories were conceived.
Once these categories were set, Tilly further argued four mechanisms allowed
categorical inequality to develop: exploitation by elites, opportunity hoarding
by nonelites, emulation, and adaptation. Over time, organizational processes
and societal decisions on access to resources would be assigned based on
these positions. Moreover, Tilly argued durable inequality depends largely on
the institutionalization of categorical pairs, rather than on individual racism
(Tilly 1998; Wood 2017).

Tilly contended the institutionalization of categorical pairs set the stage
for durable inequality in the following ways. Paired and unequal categories
were developed, which consisted of asymmetrical relations across a socially
defined line, with the usual impact of unequal exclusion of each network
controlled by the other. For example, in the U.S. experience, the most salient
historical asymmetrical relation for African Americans has been and continues to be the color line. Once formed, these categories take on a life of their
own: they can be replicated and used across a number of venues with little
cost to institutions or society in implementing them. Exploitation by elites
occurs when powerful, connected people command resources to increase
their own return, while limiting outsiders through exclusion processes. Much
of the history of African Americans has been one of racism, discrimination,
segregation, and systematic exclusion. Opportunity hoarding by nonelites
occurs when members of a categorically bounded network, that is, white
middle-class and working-class people, acquired access to a resource that
was valuable, renewable, or subject to monopolistic control, preventing others from accessing the resources. People in wealthy and powerful positions
tended to use the first of these, while people in middle-class and less powerful roles opted for the second. In Tilly's work, his focus was on social class
cleavages with respect to exploitation and opportunity hoarding. However,

these can easily be adopted to historical differences of race as the mechanisms are similar (Tilly 1998).

At an institutional level, emulation and adaptation led to further reified categories of inequality. Emulation occurs when these models are copied from one setting to another or across existing social relations. Adaptation happens as daily routines and structures are modified through time, so categorical inequalities become embedded in more organizational and societal structures. Historical experiences in these categories gave participants different and unequal preparation for performance in an organization. Much of what observers interpreted as individual differences, which create inequality, were actually the consequences of categorical organization. For these reasons, inequalities by age, citizenship, class, educational level, ethnicity, gender, race, and other apparent contradictory principles of differentiation form through similar social processes and were to an important degree organizationally interchangeable (Wood 2017). Further, the basic mechanisms, which generated categorical inequality, operated over multiple unequal outcomes such as income, wealth, power, prestige, and race. The intersections of these mechanisms created much of the distinctions we see between unequal categorical groups. Tilly concluded that durable categorical inequalities were not formed by individual decisions like racism, prejudice, or discrimination, but instead were formed by the interrelationships of social ties, networks, organizations, and finally societies, which base decisions on differential access to resources on categories (Tilly 1998). So, in the case of political and social inequities stemming from natural disasters, Tilly's work offers a convincing narrative on how early categorical decisions became embedded in institutional mechanisms. Finally, the natural disaster event itself serves as an accelerant of the existing categorical inequality by allowing institutions and organizations the ability to rely on previous set and agreed to durable inequality. Once the categories have been historically set, then reified and reproduced over time, the emulation and adaptation of said categories as the bases for decision making was a fairly easy logical extension. Such theoretical constructs then set the stage so that individual prejudicial beliefs or discriminatory actions are no longer required to reproduce social inequality.

PREVIEWING VOLUME CHAPTERS

Although critical demography and historical categorical inequality and other earlier theoretical work shaped the call for manuscripts and the initial theoretical framing of this volume, several contributing authors have developed important theoretical and empirical evidence examining the ways in which natural disasters impact political and social inequities in the United States.

The breadth and depth of the following chapters vary by approach, but each of these examine how people and communities are economically, politically, and socially impacted following natural disasters.

Loebach and Stewart argue there is a missing link in the way in which we have explored disasters in the social sciences. They argue that rather than just looking at only bonding capital as most social science work on natural does, the importance of social capital is a better explanatory factor. In their work, Loebach and Stewart stress the importance of one's social relationships or position in the social structure in delineating the ability to respond to natural disasters. Further, they contend that linking capital is a key variable in this process. In this context, linking capital is defined as vertical ties of people with less economic and political resources to others who possess these resources. While we often look at horizontal connections of people with like resources, Loebach and Stewart contend the vertical ties of asymmetrical and uneven relationships may help to explain resilience after a natural disaster. They further argue that social capital theories are less developed when applied to emergencies or natural disasters. In their work, they discuss the importance of components of social capital such as value introjection, reciprocity transactions, bounded solidarity, and enforceable trust as important variables to develop. Additionally, they advocate for revisiting the concept of embeddedness and the strength of weak ties from previous work by Mark Granovetter in the 1980s. By exploring these concepts, they then focus on four dimensions of linking capital: embeddedness, reciprocal norms, homologous values, and shared identity. They contend these can be used as axis to better elucidate recovery and resilience leading to improved impact on social inequality from natural disasters. Interestingly, Loebach and Stewart discuss how decisions of democracy and development are not made in a power vacuum, but links to class, race, and gender determine often who is worthy for aid and who is not following a natural disaster event. They conclude that state-society literature could be helpful were it to be applied to natural disasters research once coupled with linking capital attributes.

While Loebach and Stewart examine the importance of linking capital and its relevance to outcomes during natural disasters, Paul Adams questions the degree of democracy in the United States in that many citizens are deprived of the right to vote through a decentralized system of rules on criminal disenfranchisement, registration barriers, and hurdles to ballot access. Although these barriers affect Americans from minority groups and lower social classes disproportionately already, these issues tend to exacerbate the impact of decentralized voting systems on people affected by natural disasters, emergency events, or public health threats. Decentralized voting systems at the federal, state, and local levels amplify existing social and economic inequality. While voter access, consistent voting rules, and voter registration are negatively impacted by hyper-decentralization, the prevalence of natural disasters acts as gasoline on a smoldering fire. Adams further argues institutional and structural variables play a role in how registering of voters, party affiliation, and casting of ballots takes place. He contends institutional barriers are an important and significant causal mechanism in the suppression of disadvantaged citizens and this becomes magnified during times of crises and natural disasters.

Adams elaborates on the growing evidence of scholarship indicating how levels of decentralization in the American system of elections and voting administration are tied to the exclusion of minority and economically disadvantaged voters. He indicates that institutionalized systems of decentralization and disenfranchisement are strongly connected to the seeds of categorical inequality discussed earlier in this chapter. Although categorical inequality is already at work in neighborhoods of people of color and those of lower socioeconomic status, natural disasters makes inequality worse by accelerating trends in elections and voting systems.

Adams concludes substantial decentralization of American elections and voting systems lead to unequal outcomes, especially during turbulent times. However, Amilcar Antonio Barreto explores the worthiness of people experiencing natural disasters. Barreto takes on the notion of what it means to be a citizen in American society, and how this differs by several key characteristics. He contends that there is an expectation that government will assist during natural disaster events, but little attention is paid to the competing notions of citizenship. In this chapter, Barreto examines the federal government response to Hurricane Maria in 2017 to see how racialization of citizenship matters. In this case, the Trump Administration actually blamed Puerto Rico for much of its own problems by citing economic mismanagement over time as the root of the economic problems. Additionally, the Trump Administration downplayed the severity of the event, and chastised local leaders for their efforts. Barreto argues this uneven response is due to the perceived lack of worthiness of Puerto Ricans as American citizens. Further, he contends the 2016 PROMESA Act to impose fiscal oversight after decreasing the amount of federal funding for manufacturing and economic growth was an initial step in reducing the worth of Puerto Ricans. Then, when Hurricane Maria hit Puerto Rico directly, there were already infrastructural problems with electricity, food, medicine, and refrigeration across the island. Interestingly, public opinion polls at the time showed that only half of Americans believed Puerto Ricans were even U.S. citizens, and Barreto contends this ignorance contributed to allowing the Trump Administration to paint Puerto Ricans as the undeserving poor. He further adds that this narrative is typical of the Trump Administration: shift blame to others, mention debt or some other infrastructural problem, but then take no responsibility for any federal relief efforts. American compassion is only reserved for real Americans. Barreto argues convincingly that Trump's comparative disaster logic is to separate brown and black Americans from white ones, and then create a dialogue where only the white Americans are deserving. In addition, Trump also groups citizen Puerto Ricans with non-citizen Mexicans nationals and then would make claims about the groups as if these were the same. Barreto further argues that the U.S. media contributed to these characteristics first during Hurricane Katrina with African Americans, and then during Hurricane Maria with Puerto Rican American citizens. The creation of an anti-citizens rhetoric coupled with racializing geography creates a different, lesser type of citizenship based on race and power in the case of Puerto Ricans.

Barreto makes some important and relevant conclusions that align well with the earlier discussion of critical demography and categorical inequality. First, he argues that racialized Puerto Ricans are deemed less worthy than their white counterparts. By placing whites and non-whites in two separate and unequal categories, the stage is then set for institutions and organizations to use the categories to reward or punish in terms of power and privileges. Next, he contends that national identity and authenticity is limited to whites only. In the context of Hurricane Maria, Puerto Ricans were treated like noncitizens and undeserving of compassion or empathy. Barreto concludes that responses to natural disasters are less about the actual damage or loss of life, but more about the perceived worthiness of the people involved. In the case of Puerto Rico, these Americans were not deemed worthy. We cannot look at their race, ethnicity, gender, or citizenship status of Puerto Ricans during Hurricane Maria without considering how the categories were formed and how power and resources were allocated initially, and then how these decisions impacted systemic and institutionalized differences later during a natural disaster event.

In her work examining perceptions of reconstruction following a tornado in Tuscaloosa, Alabama in 2011, Ariane Prohaska examines how a low-income neighborhood was hit hard by a natural disaster by conducting qualitative interviews with community residents. The focus of her work is residents' perceptions of rebuilding and reconstruction following the tornado. She argues from a community and social vulnerability perspective that those of lower social status tend to have poorer outcomes and are subsequently not viewed as stakeholders in the rebuilding process. She also contends that negative attitudes toward reconstruction post-disaster vary by class, race, and ethnicity. In this chapter, the analysis is focused on themes related to recovery and reconstruction problems that participants attribute to the city government, neighborhood changes, and shifts in community demographics. Three themes about recovery and reconstruction emerged as a result of her interviews with residents. The first of these is residents were dissatisfied with the city's response to the crisis. Residents were also frustrated with the speed of the rebuilding process of the city. Finally, residents expressed unhappiness with changes to the city landscape, such as gentrification, slow rebuilding efforts, or the lack of businesses returning to the area.

As a result of this research, Prohaska discusses several important contributions of her examination of the tornado which affected Tuscaloosa, Alabama in 2011. Although this research highlights the importance of measuring satisfaction of the recovery process, Prohaska contends no previous research has addressed resident satisfaction with recovery efforts from a qualitative perspective. Importantly, she discovered notable differentiated community perceptions of the rebuilding process. She found that vulnerable individuals in marginalized communities expressed the highest levels of dissatisfaction on rebuilding. Whereas middle-class tornado survivors worried about the changing city landscape and building codes, individuals of lower incomes and people of color felt distrust toward city officials. Well-situated individuals were mostly concerned with bouncing back to their pre-storm economic status, and any impediments to their return to normalcy caused these residents stress. On the other hand, marginalized survivors were concerned with their survival; these participants were struggling to get back on their feet and felt that the slow rebuilding of their communities was hindering their capacities to meet basic needs. This case study of Tuscaloosa, Alabama shows further support for social vulnerability and community vulnerability perspectives of disaster recovery.

Looking at another perspective relevant to the impact of natural disasters, Pamela Koch and Dennis Feaster examine hurricanes and the impact on the criminal justice system. Specifically, they looked at decisions in Polk County, Florida to not allow nonviolent criminal access to disaster shelters during Hurricane Harvey in 2017. In their chapter, Koch and Feaster examine structural barriers impacting reentry for offenders generally, sex offenders specifically, and the intellectually disabled. They argue systemic and structural barriers often prevent this group of offenders from being able successfully reintegrate into society. They discuss the growth of incarceration and the use of three strikes laws, as mechanisms to keep nonviolent offenders incarcerated for long periods of time. Koch and Feaster contend that reentry issues are a significant problem for these nonviolent offenders. Reentry issue such as housing of released offenders, diminished community and neighborhood resource connections, voting, the treatment of people of color in the community and historical disenfranchisement after incarceration are key themes in their narrative. They argue that natural disasters tend to make these events more difficult for released offenders to overcome. Evidence from Polk County indicates living with a warrant during Hurricane Harvey made it onerous for those living with warrant or with a sex offender status. Punitive measures as well as sex offender registries were a deterrent to the offender population seeking help during this natural disaster event. Additionally, Koch and Feaster contend those with intellectual disabilities with any ties to sex offenses were virtually ignored by disaster relief organizations and local government decision makers. In the case of Florida, they argue there has been a great deal of over disenfranchisement of released offenders in a concerted effort to prevent them from voting in elections. During the hurricane, there was no real reintegration of these residents, but instead remaining barriers kept them largely isolated from relief efforts. They conclude that disaster responses accelerate these trends for offenders, and this topic needs more attention in the criminal justice literature.

Tim Holler and Renee Lamphere examine media framing, crime, and the role categorical inequality plays in the impact of natural disasters. They begin by exploring the role of natural disasters and crime through the lens of existing categorical inequality. Holler and Lamphere contend that post-disaster perceptions of criminal activity affects categories differently. So as discussed earlier in this chapter, categorical inequality has initially been set, and then the natural disaster event exacerbates or accelerates the degree of inequality. Holler and Lamphere further argue that "just system" laws are executed differentially based on status, race, and gender. They make the case that these unequal categories intersect with the criminal justice system in such a way that the criminal justice system uses these categories to sort offenders. Further, they contend that race and class set up a system where criminal behavior is dichotomized into acceptable versus unacceptable crime. While this often mirrors the distinction between white collar and street crimes, it looks eerily similar to distinctions based on categories of race, class, and gender. In their work, they discuss the ways in which media focus and government response concentrate on constricted range of crimes: namely violent street criminal offenses. Holler and Lamphere argue that media portrayals of crime feed the differential and inappropriate responses for those already marginalized or othered in society. Media has an implicit role in framing categorical inequality and then organizing how institutional responses to crime are crafted during disasters. Post-disaster decision making then becomes institutionalized through the processes of adaptation and emulation of accelerated categorical inequality. They contend media portrayal of stereotypes that the poor are responsible for their plight coupled with oversimplification of complicated issues by media continues to compound the link between blackness and crime. Rather than concentrating on legislative action to correct institutional or structural problems, Holler and Lamphere argue policing has become the preferred method in times of crisis.

Further, Holler and Lamphere argue there were similarities of Hurricanes Katrina and Maria in terms of institutional media framing. Media coverage of events had embedded categorical inequality in it as it framed similar actions as either blacks "looting" or whites "finding supplies." It was in fact the same behavior but labeled through the lens of categorical inequality in different ways. Also important was the use of the label "refugee" that was applied to blacks during Hurricane Katrina, and allowed them to be defined as an othering group people, not worthy of compassion or assistance. Holler and Lamphere espouse and illuminate several key points ignored by media framing of such events. First, the poor are simply more affected by disasters. Next, other risk factors such as race, ethnicity, age, and disability compounded by poverty allow categories of individuals to be placed in less advantageous positions by the media. Rather than focusing on these demographic characteristics, they contend interpersonal violence and crimes, like child abuse, domestic violence should really receive more attention in news reporting. Victimization of women during natural disasters is an important but understudied area. Finally, white collar crime is not reported on as these do not shape the media narrative of focus on street crimes. Holler and Lamphere conclude the role of media in portraying events reinforces categorical inequality. Although inequality existed in New Orleans prior to Hurricane Katrina and in Puerto Rico before Hurricane Maria, systemic race and class biases were reinforced and reified by media coverage. This allowed for viewers to see these victims as violent criminals, rather than a deserving resident population. In the narrative of both events, the media characterized survivors as refugees, criminals, and second-class citizens or foreigners not worthy of governmental assistance or support.

Throughout this edited volume, chapter contributors examine the impact of natural disasters on political and social inequities. Some scholars view events through a theoretical, methodological, qualitative, or quantitative lens. Regardless of the initial paradigm used, each of these pieces works toward enhancing our understanding of the ways in which disaster impact people in communities. As we developed the initial call for manuscripts, it was our goal and hope to develop an edited volume looking at nuances in how the demographic, economic, political, and social lives of people are impacted first by a natural disaster, and then by the responses of others. We believe the scholars in this edited volume have delivered the degree of nuances needed to move this literature and forward. As we consider the long-term ramifications of COVID-19 on the political and social inequities in communities, it is our desire that this volume serve as a starting point for those discussions.

REFERENCES

Horton, Hayward. "Critical Demography: The Paradigm of the Future." *Sociological Forum* 14 (1999): 363–367.

Tilly, Charles. *Durable Inequality.* Berkeley, CA: University of California Press, 1998.

Wood, Geoffrey L. "Accelerated Categorical Inequality: New Orleans in the Eye of the Storm." In *After the Storm: Militarization, Occupation, and Segregation in Post-Katrina America*, eds. Lori Latrice Martin, Hayward Derrick Horton, and Kenneth Fasching-Varner. Santa Barbara, CA: Praeger, 2016.

Wood, Geoffrey L. "Seventeen Years Later: Revisiting the Critical Demography Paradigm to Examine Public Education in American Schools." In *Race, Population Studies, and America's Public Schools: A Critical Demography Perspective*, eds. Hayward Derrick Horton, Lori Latrice Martin, and Kenneth Fasching-Varner. Lanham, MD: Lexington Books, 2017.

Wood, Geoffrey L. "Historical Categorical Inequality: The Creation of Two Segregated Cities Within an Urban Center." In *#BRoken Promises, Black Deaths, & Blue Ribbons: Understanding, Complicating, and Transcending Police—Community Violence*, eds. Kenneth Fasching-Varner, Kerri Tobin, and Stephen Lentz. Leiden: Brill-Sense, 2018.

Wood, Geoffrey L. "Racialized Categorical Inequality: Elaborating Educational Theory to Explain African American Disparities in Public Schools." *Issues in Race & Society: An Interdisciplinary Global Journal* 8 (2019): 177–196.

Chapter 2

The Missing Link in
Disaster Social Science

Peter Loebach and Julie Stewart

This chapter integrates the empirical concerns of disaster research with an underapplied dimension of a central sociological concept: social capital. Few concepts in the social sciences have attracted as much attention in recent years.[1] Although a lengthier discussion on social capital follows later, Portes—one of the more significant sociologists to develop this term—suggests that the first step in understanding social capital is to distinguish it from what it is not. He argues, "Whereas economic capital is in people's bank accounts and human capital is inside their heads, social capital inheres in the structure of their relationships" (Portes 1998, 7). Accordingly, we broadly define social capital as the capacity to mobilize resources based on one's social relationships or one's position with the social structure. In a collective setting, we study how shared norms, networks, common values and solidarity enhance general well-being and socially positive outcomes (Portes 1998, 2000).

An important innovation our research advances is a better understanding of an under-studied form of social capital: linking capital. The two major forms of social capital—bonding and bridging—are now well-known. From a network perspective, bonding capital is the strong ties that connect immediate family, friends and neighbors (Gittel and Vidal 1998; Putnam 2000). In economic development, bonding capital is often central to the survival strategies of the very poor (Bebbington 1999; Stack 1974). Bridging capital encompasses the cross-cutting, weaker ties between people from different groups, whether geographical, ethnic, religious, or racial (Granovetter 1973; Narayan 2000). As Putnam and Goss (2002) have argued, regions that feature strong bridging capital are less likely to experience intense ethnic, racial, or religious conflict. They are more likely to unite around civic initiatives on a national or transnational scale. Bridging capital connects people across disparate social cleavages, finding common cause in an issue or an identity that may transcend differences of racial or ethnic identity or socioeconomic position. But, even "strong" bridging capital has limits.

In contrast, linking capital applies to the vertical ties between people with fewer economic resources and political power and those who have precisely the opposite advantages (Szreter 2002; Szreter and Woolcock 2004; Woolcock 1998). In the most cited definition of linking capital, Szreter and Woolcock (2004) argue that it features "the norms of respect and networks of trusting relationships between people who are interacting across explicit, formal or institutionalized power or authority gradients in society" (655). We elaborate further on these dimensions later in the chapter. Examples of linking capital include relationships between a community and government actors, representatives of national or international NGOs, or members of private institutions. These relationships are typically unequal and asymmetrical. But, they may be precisely the kind of relationships that facilitate survival, recovery and resilience following disasters and mass emergencies. For reasons that we elucidate in this chapter, we argue that a better understanding of linking capital may clarify the causal mechanisms behind post-disaster failures and may elucidate the building blocks of relationships that contribute to post-disaster resilience.

In her review of disaster research, Tierney (2007) notes, "Sociological research on disasters in the United States has remained largely isolated from major theoretical developments in sociology" (2007, 516), largely because research has been more concerned with solving problems than advancing theory. To understand the role of linking capital in social responses to disasters and mass emergencies, discussion begins with a short overview of the social capital literature, first highlighting the major criticisms that surround this approach. We then explore illustrative examples of how it contributes to development and democratization on a community and national scale. The social capital literature in the areas of development and democratization provides us a conceptual framework from which we can glean insights into vertical relationships, and the critical dimension of the quality of these relationships, which we argue are pertinent to the area of disasters and mass emergencies. We explore the literature on social capital and disasters/mass emergencies, highlighting the specific leverage that comes from the linking capital perspective. Discussion then turns to a critical exploration of the history of emergency management in the United States. Importantly, this history highlights the problems of a centralized and hierarchical command-and-control emergency response system. This U.S. style of emergency response attracted broad criticisms and it began to change. For a time, it seemed that disaster and emergency response systems had decentralized, turning to communities for leadership, information, communication and collaboration. But the September 11 attacks reversed this community turn and disaster and emergency response styles returned to their previous form characterized by uniformity, compliance, and subordination. A next pivotal moment was Hurricane Katrina, a tragedy that compelled further systemic change, including implementation of *Whole Community*, a national approach to emergency management that, at least in theory, emphasizes community engagement, coordination, and shared responsibility. We argue that understanding the social dimensions of mass emergencies and natural disasters—with a focus on the role of linking capital—could be an important corrective to transform emergency management in the United States.

SOCIAL CAPITAL: CAUSE FOR CELEBRATION OR CONDEMNATION?

Social capital scholarship has generated significant attention for three reasons. First, it connects with central sociological concepts such as social integration and solidarity (Lin et al. 2001; Fine 2001). Second, its social networks focus helps bridge the pernicious chasm between structure and agency, between micro- and macro-analysis (Coleman 1990; Emirbayer and Goodwin 1994). Third, it applies to a wide range of social phenomena. Researchers have credited social capital for reigning in teenage pregnancy and juvenile delinquency and keeping at-risk youth in school (Browning et al. 2005; Crane 1991; Zhou and Bankston 1996). Individual social capital helps shape access to employment, occupational mobility, and entrepreneurial success (Granovetter 1973; Portes 1987). High participation in civic associations has long been linked to the quality of a nation's democracy (Paxton 2002; Putnam 1993, 2000). And, in the development realm, social capital may be the "missing link" that explains the difference between harmonious, prosperous and cohesive communities versus societies plagued by conflict, distrust and poverty (Grootaert 1998).

However, social capital research has been more ubiquitous than theoretically consistent (Moody and White 2003) and detractors have increasingly questioned the link between social capital and positive social outcomes such as community development and political change. By reflecting on their theoretical similarities, we highlight three central criticisms of social capital as a coherent concept: (1) unintended consequences and/or overlooked drawbacks; (2) philosophical objections; (3) methodological and/or ontological concerns.

One criticism points out that community outcomes associated with social capital are not all positive. Social capital may have externalities, and therefore fostering social capital can produce unintended consequences, such as heightening internal stratification. A community-based project in rural India intended to improve farming practices among impoverished farmers is illustrative: even as well-connected farmers benefited from the project—both socially and economically—the project was less successful in attracting the participation of socially marginalized, relatively poorer farmers—(Kumar and Corbridge 2002). Cleaver's (2005) research in Tanzania sustained these findings. In a similar vein, Portes and his collaborators have identified the "darker side" of social capital, the overlooked drawbacks that often accompany densely networked communities. They may exclude outsiders who could bring valuable resources—monetary, informational or cultural—to a group (Portes 1998; Portes and Landolt 2000). While Min Zhou (2004) demonstrates how social capital rich ethnic enclaves of Chinatown and Koreatown in Los Angeles bestow benefits on members otherwise marginalized from opportunities in the American mainstream, Roger Waldinger highlights how such enclaves also produce racialized closure, where access to economic opportunities is impeded for non co-ethnics (Waldinger 2010). Tightly-knit, but impoverished communities can also enhance downward-leveling norms because part of their identity and coherence is based on the alleged impossibility of success. This forces ambitious people to escape their communities in search of success, as Bourgois (1995) illustrated in his research on the South Bronx.

A second, more philosophical criticism argues that a focus on social capital depoliticizes poverty—that it takes the state off the hook, overlooks history and rests an overly critical gaze on the individual rather than on structure. As Edwards et al. (2003) have argued, social capital's reliance on associational relationships to explain prosperity and poverty legitimizes a policy focus on individuals and their networks, thus shifting responsibility from the economy to society and from government to the individual. In Fine's words, by "raising the virtues of civil society to pedestal status, social capital has studiously ignored questions of power, conflict, the elite, and the systematic imperatives of contemporary capitalism" (2002, 796). This inevitably leads us back to blaming poor people for being poor and other recycled versions of the 1960s culture of poverty arguments (Schafft and Brown 2003). Thus, it is important to keep public policy and state actors at the center of our analysis. But government rarely acts alone. It is only through investigating the interactions between individuals, groups and the state that we develop a full picture of how linking capital operates and why it may be important to disasters research.

Finally, prominent objections revolve around methodological and ontological concerns. When applied to any unit beyond the individual, some contend that social capital gets drawn into a tautological vortex. Portes has argued that as a collective concept, "social capital is simultaneously cause and effect" (Portes 1998, 19). Portes' critique of Putnam's explanation of politics and economic development in Italy illustrates this point. As he put it, civic behaviors compose civic communities, which foster wealth creation and functional societies. In contrast, noncivic communities, comprised of noncivic actors, create and deepen poverty, corruption and inefficiency. To express it less abstractly, an absence of corrupt behavior—on the part of citizens and public officials alike—tends to correlate with wealthier economies and more efficient governments. The converse is also true. But, because it is difficult to retroactively disentangle these factors to demonstrate causality, measures of civic behavior become synonymous with wealth. Eventually, the original problem gets relabeled, and scholars search for the simultaneous existence of social capital, wealth and political efficacy to demonstrate their relationship without fully explaining its nature (Portes and Landolt 2000). Consequently, the cause and effect become interchangeable.

To escape the tautological vortex of social capital research, we recommend that research follow Portes' prescription. First, one must separate the concept—theoretically and empirically—from its alleged effect. Second, research should demonstrate that the presence of social capital precedes outcomes. At a minimum, research much acknowledge that sometimes what is taken as causal is actually a strong correlation. Relatedly, one should identify the existence of other variables that may work alongside social capital indicators to contribute to notable outcomes. Finally, research that effectively uses the social capital framework must systematically identify the historical origins of community social capital (Portes 1998).

If researchers follow this prescription, the resulting analysis will be more robust and applicable. This does not address all of the other—still valid—criticisms of social capital, but it is a useful start to explaining how social capital can help unite communities during a crisis and pursue longer-term political and economic goals. It also sheds light on the opposite phenomenon: how a lack of social capital depletes unity and erodes effective responses to crises. In that vein, it is helpful to review the four critical attributes of social capital by returning to the work of Portes and his collaborators. They identified four modes of social capital—drawing from classical sociological concepts—that help us get closer to this question of the content and quality of the ties that make crucial differences in people's lives.

The first is "value introjection," which draws on the Durkheimian tradition to argue that certain values, moral imperatives and commitments precede contractual relations and inform individual goals outside of strictly instrumental motivations. The over-arching value of caring for one's neighbor is a classic example of this modal value. The second mode is "reciprocity transactions," a diffuse form of interaction guided by norms and obligations that emerge through personalized networks of exchanges (Granovetter

1973). Neighbors trading favors or friends sharing information about job oppotunities are examples of this type of action. The third mode is "bounded solidarity," which draws from work by Marx and Engels to argue that adverse circumstances can create group cohesion. While they had class conflict and labor strikes in mind, the adversity, challenges and tragedy that accompany natural disaster could theoretically function in the same way. However, we should acknowledge that no one identity claims the entirety of a person; the intersectionality of class, ethnicity, race and gender are all germane in shaping how people connect with fellow survivors and who is deemed "deserving" of assistance. Finally, the Weberian tradition provides us with the fourth mode of social capital, the notion of "enforceable trust." This is the idea that formal institutions and particular group settings use different mechanisms for ensuring compliance with rules of conduct. In emergency situations, adhering to agreed-upon rules can literally mean the difference between life and death.

Before turning to this type of mass emergency or disaster, we touch on illustrative evidence in the development and democratization literature, arguing that lessons learned from efforts to develop or democratize a community can help us conceptually map the relevant social dynamics that also come into play during mass emergencies and disasters.

RESTORING THE MISSING LINKS: AN EXPANDED VIEW OF SOCIAL CAPITAL RESEARCH

Putnam's work is foundational to any argument about the role of social capital in development. While it is not without its criticisms (including those explored in this chapter) his (1993) study of divergent development outcomes in Italy highlighted the importance of dense horizontal ties between civil society and state actors. Like-minded research explored how social capital helps reduce poverty by encouraging more accountable, autonomous and effective states. The resultant "developmental states"—such as Japan, South Korea and Singapore—are characterized by "embedded autonomy." Concrete social ties bind the state to society to enhance communication, even as state actors maintain sufficient autonomy to pursue independent goals (Collier 1998; Evans 1995). Ideally, state–society synergy results, creating a complementarity between an engaged government, capable of utilizing economy of scale advantages, and mobilized communities, which are uniquely positioned to monitor projects, deliver sanctions, provide local knowledge and negotiate class compromise (Das Gupta et al. 2004; Evans 1996; Heller 1996).

Even in states that function poorly, there is evidence that community-level social capital can enhance economic prosperity and collective well-being. For example, in their Bolivian study, Grootaert and Narayan (2004) demonstrated that households with higher levels of civic participation had a lower probability of being poor. Okten and Osili (2004) similarly found that regular participation in local meetings increased the likelihood that people were aware of new credit sources in Indonesia. Association generates prosperity by enhancing information flow and coordinating collective practices. As demonstrated in places as diverse as China, the Philippines and Brazil, group membership increases trust and the probability that social sanctions will limit anti-social behavior (Kumar and Corbridge 2002; Das Gupta et al. 2004).

More recently, scholarship has combined these two levels (nation-state and community) by exploring how linking social capital creates elective affinities between communities and the nation-states in which they are embedded. In their study of small business resilience after Hurricane Katrina et al. (2018) identify how businesses that were more embedded in their communities, that is, had larger stocks of bridging capital, were more able to reach out to federal agencies providing assistance (Federal Emergency Management Agency and the Small Business Administration). Ten years after this natural disaster, these more resilient businesses were serving as crucial linking capital for their communities, connecting federal funds and knowledge with the provision of local services and employment opportunities. Conversely, in their study of economic development in the Osa and Golfito region of Costa Rica, Hunt et al. (2015) argue that development opportunities were lost due to the lack of bridging and linking forms of social capital. Even in the face of exogenous investment opportunities, they attribute the region's persistent development challenges to precisely these gaps.

The celebrated case of Porto Alegre suggests that social capital can also produce political transformation, even democratization. This Brazilian city of 1.3 million people was historically a bastion of clientelism—a system of closed-door decision-making and favor exchanges—with an infamous predatory political culture (Abers 1998, 2000). Yet following the Worker's Party electoral victory in 1988, the city transformed itself into a model of transparent and participatory governance. During the annual open budget meetings, upwards of 14,000 people helped decide the distribution of municipal funds. Over time, people began to vote for more equitable resource distribution rather than their own individualistic interests, producing decisions that typically favored poorer districts over wealthier ones.

The cumulative success of the budget proceedings was facilitated by the strategic intervention of several activists. They attracted participants, facilitated meetings, and proposed compromises (Abers 1998). For example, in one district, a "cadre of committed activists" drew upon relationships formed during the 1980s with political dissidents and progressive clergy to help neighborhoods elect officials and learn the value of cooperating over competing (Baiocchi 2005). This resulted in a greater focus on district-wide issues and translated into more successful development outcomes. The funded projects—paving roads, installing electricity or providing water—had a completion rate of nearly 100 percent. This success did not go unnoticed. Between 1997 and 2004, at least 200 Brazilian cities experimented with the open budget model, attempting to implement the social capital principles behind Porto Alegre's success story (Baiocchi 2005). At the heart of this success was the ability of these activists to link poorer, less powerful constituents with civic and religious leaders who could effectively negotiate on their behalf. A number of additional case studies highlight a similar function at play in political transformation, even as they do not consistently use the term "linking capital" (Berenschot 2010; Fox and Brown 1998; Heller 1996; Krishna 2002; Narayan 2000; Woolcock 2001).

And while we acknowledge that linking capital is no panacea for solving all problems of development or democracy—see Rubin's (2016) thorough account of the ways that operationalizing linking capital to answer political questions fails to the do the job—we suggest that part of the problem lies in researchers picking and choosing which dimensions of linking capital to study. Some focus on trust, others on norms of reciprocity. A more effective approach would include the four dimensions–embeddedness, reciprocal norms, homologous values, and a shared identity. Focusing on these four dimensions—rather than choosing only one axis of discussion—has greater potential to elucidate how linking capital actually operates in disaster contexts. It can illuminate the types of relationships that lead to recovery and resilience, while also exposing those relationships that reinforce existing inequalities. We argue that studying the presence of linking capital in disasters research—operationalized fully—would advance theory and improve praxis.

To date, the published research on linking capital reveals that this is a fledgling field, but one that could speak directly to the dilemmas of disaster and mass emergency research.[2] We need to better understand its role in disasters, which has suffered from important "blind spots" (Tierney 2007, 515). Disaster researchers have consistently criticized relief efforts in which "top-down" aid organizations failed to coordinate with affected communities (Drabek 1999; Dynes 1974); however, the disasters literature has largely failed to identify the lack of linking capital as a partial explanation. In their 2011 book, Ride and Bretherton argue that "Disasters are interesting because they tell us something about human behavior. The disaster calls upon communities to respond and exploring these community responses provides information about how a community functions, treats outsiders, and rises to new challenges" (2011, 7). The persistent wide variation in response and recovery outcomes, across and within nations, compels the development of an explanatory conceptual framework of community and state relations. Such a framework could inform policies in an era of escalating human and environmental losses from disaster events.

RECOVERING FROM DISASTER: WHAT A DIFFERENCE SOCIAL CAPITAL MAKES

The vulnerabilities approach to studying natural disasters denaturalizes disaster, placing emphasis on the cause of disasters in pre-existing community conditions (Blaikie et al. 1994; Cannon 1994). Researchers commonly invoke the term "community resilience" to explain why some communities unite under times of tragedy and effectively engage in collective action. Community-level social capital has often helped explain this phenomenon. Numerous comparative studies have suggested that communities with strong bridging and bonding social capital fare better in disaster recovery than communities relatively weak in these capitals (Norris et al. 2007). Nakagawa and Shaw's (2004) analysis of Indian communities affected by an earthquake in 2001 found that bridging and bonding social capitals were robust predictors of recovery success. Similarly, Buckland and Rahman's (1999) comparative study of Canadian communities affected by a devastating flood of the Red River found community-level social capital promoted recovery. Aldrich's (2010) study of a 1995 earthquake in Kobe, Japan found similarly positive social capital effects.

While these studies focus on *existing* intra-community social capital, the literature also finds that social capital increases in communities *following* disasters. Dynes (2006) identifies two forms of social capital that regularly amplify in post-disaster communities. First, altruistic norms proliferate as communities suspend many usual activities to prioritize victim care and community recovery. For example, Nakagawa and Shaw (2004) found that following the Kobe, Japan 1995 earthquake, heightened altruism emerged in affected areas as property owners downplayed private interests to prioritize the safety of the community. Further, they documented the formation of "Machizukuri," or town development organizations. These organizations wedded existing civic organizations with academics, city planners and local government, resulting in synergetic, coordinated relief efforts. Mimaki and Shaw (2007) found that in rural Japanese communities affected by torrential rains, bridging and bonding social capital grew in the form of greater coordination between fire departments and a general increase in communities' collective concern for their children.

Second, disasters may intensify a community's sense of collective identity. Individuals increasingly identify as members of a community and prioritize collective obligations. For example, Cox and Perry's (2011) ethnographic study of two rural communities affected by a wildfire in British Columbia described a post-disaster process in which camaraderie and regional community identity increased. They argued that communities can deepen their attachment to a place or even "forge" new social capitals following disasters. Chamlee-Wright and Storr (2009) observed that following Hurricane Katrina, an intense attachment, strong community identification and a collective narrative emerged in the St. Bernard area of New Orleans. The narrative stressed St. Bernard's history of collectively overcoming hardships, and it contributed to community members remaining in their damaged community to help it recover.

Contrasted with the generally positive aforementioned social phenomenon in the context of disasters—heightened collective community identity, pooling of social resources—Aldrich (2009) notes detrimental social dimensions of disasters, including group exclusion and intensive group affiliation being only internal to groups. The intense bonding capital that can be so beneficial to in-group members may be at the expense of other groups that become excluded from critical benefits and mutual resources. Potentially, this phenomenon can be a source of unequal recovery outcomes and exacerbated community inequality following disaster events. Elliot et al. (2010) document the outcomes associated with scarce and exclusive social capital in the case of Hurricane Katrina. Many members of the Lower Ninth Ward, predominantly lower-income and African American, were unable to draw upon social resources to facilitate their response to the event—particularly critical were social connections that could be tapped to access evacuation housing and transportation. Furthermore, the disaster brought not heightened, but decreased community identification over time, because processes of displacement, where members were haphazardly airlifted to various locales around the country, effectively separated community members geographically. In this case, low-levels of social capital stymied community members' ability to respond and recover to the event; but furthermore, the disaster had the effect of severing community relations, thereby further decreasing members' social resources. This case vividly demonstrates how if not matched by bridging capital—the social capital that spans socioeconomic and racial/ethnic lines—scarce and exclusive bonding capital can be a cause of disaster inequality.

While research on disasters has documented a generally positive relationship between bonding and bridging social capital and ability to respond and recover, until recently, it has not utilized the concept of linking capital. This exclusion may have resulted in an inability to fully understand the role that outsiders can play in disaster response and may help explain the sometimes ambiguous, even contradictory interpretations of the intersection of disasters and social capital. While Buckland and Rahman's study found a generally positive relationship between a community's level of social capital and disaster recovery, they also qualified that "Social capital can be a double-edged sword" (2002, 187). When the provincial government mandated a flood evacuation, one town with a high level of social capital engaged in in-fighting, stalling the evacuation. This delay could have proven disastrous. The authors suggested that the in-fighting arose from distrust of a top-down, disconnected provincial government. But they did not integrate this qualification into their social capital explanation. Cox and Perry's (2011) study featured a similar case. Following a heightened level of post-disaster unification in one community, its cohesion fractured over a dispute about the distribution of donated aid from outside sources. If we reconsider these cases from a linking capital perspective, these complications and contradictions become explicable. In both situations, collective, coordinated action faltered when the community interacted with outside actors, evidencing the importance of linking capital in terms of the quality of community-level "vertical" ties with supra-community actors.

These case studies underscore why research on the role of social capital in shaping disaster response and recovery has sometimes been contradictory, even incomplete. Linking capital's more holistic vision—with a focus on connections that feature embeddedness, reciprocal norms, homologous values, and a shared identity—illuminates the key dimensions relevant to this field. But after breaking linking capital down to its components, we need to look for the mechanisms that generate solidarity and a shared identity; we need to better understand the process of developing reciprocal norms. We need to explore the balance between sanctions and rewards and its role in creating enforceable trust. And we need to be able to delineate how individually held values become collective values. Failure to engage in this level of analysis contributes to problems of practice and understanding, as this brief history of emergency management in the U.S. will detail.

COMMUNITY EMERGENCY MANAGEMENT IN THE UNITED STATES: COMMAND AND CONTROL OR COLLABORATE AND COOPERATE?

From the droughts and windstorms of the dustbowl, to the great floods of the Mississippi in the 1930s, to the partial melt down of Three Mile Island reactor, to the terrorist attacks of 9/11, the state is the actor with primary responsibility for disaster management in the United States. State-led disaster relief in the United States occurred as early as the turn of the nineteenth century, even preceding expansion of the modern welfare state (Dauber 2005). In fact, state responsibility for disaster relief was a precedent cited to justify expansion of the American welfare state during policy debates of the late nineteenth century and early twentieth century (Dauber 2005).

Advanced, formalized systems of emergency management with coordination at the local level, beyond traditional first responder roles (e.g., fire, EMS, police), emerged in the mid-twentieth century in the context of preparations for a looming threat of the time: a nuclear attack (Dynes 1994). In 1951, a suite of federal policies were signed into law by President Truman for the dual purpose of civil defense and disaster management. Civil defense authorities believed preparations for a nuclear attack would be insufficient if carried out at the national level alone. Under the Federal Civil Defense Act of 1950, federal resources were allocated to developing local level emergency management capacities (Boyer and Cohen 1951). Given that the threat of nuclear attack was an extension of international warfare, it was logical that the military, with all its developed capacities, would head management of this hazard (Drabek 1986; Dynes 1994; Waugh and Streib 2006). Communities were designated civil defense directors, and because emergency planning was all but unknown to those outside a military background, the directors commonly came from a military background. This legislation instituted a a militaristic system of local level emergency management which followed orders and a management template dictated from the national level, where authority was vested in the Federal Civil Defense Administration and the Office of Defense Mobilization (Wilson and Oyola-Yemaiel 2001). It was a system that extended to the local level, but was ultimately top-down, with federal-level experts mandating a uniform set of preparations to be carried out under a logic of command and control (Drabek 2007; Dynes 1994). It would become termed the top-down bureaucratic model of emergency management (Waugh and Streib 2006).

Although preparing for a nuclear attack was the focus of mid-twentieth century emergency management, the system served a second role. It was charged with managing other major hazards, natural and technological (Dynes 1983). Given that many of the functions that requirement fulfillment in the event of a disaster—whether a bombing, earthquake, or coastal erosion—require similar types of responses, a central source of resources can efficiently offer a deep well of resources and technological expertise for a variety of events. The complex and severe problems that accompany disasters can easily overwhelm local capacities (Rubin 2016). In a twist of circumstance and bureaucratic persistence, as the twentieth century progressed, a decline in threat of enemy attack, contrasted by a relentless series of natural events, led to the secondary mission of the civil defense offices supplanting the first (Drabek 2007; Dynes 1983).

Disaster scholars of the mid to late twentieth century, many associated with the Disaster Research Center, pointed out numerous problems with the bureaucratic model of disaster management and its twentieth century manifestation, the local civil defense offices. They noted consistently fragmented, uncoordinated, and "typically problem plagued" (Quarantelli 1988, 3) efforts to manage large scale events. The supposed front line of a national system of disaster management, local civil defense offices held hodgepodge positions in systems of governance; their integration with other community organizations was generally poor (Drabek 1987; Quarantelli 1988). Other public and private community emergency groups tended to view the offices with skepticism and kept their distance. As a result of their poor embedding in local communities, local civil defense offices inconsistently accomplished even the simplest functions of disaster management at the community level that required coordination, such as establishing emergency operations centers or engaging in disaster preparedness planning (Quarantelli 1988). The more bedeviling functions of managing hazards that involve complex trade-offs and deep integration with community planning (e.g., mitigation and recovery planning) were off the table completely.

Beyond the problem of the poor embedding of the civil defense offices in local communities, scholars identified repeated cases in which systems of emergency management failed to connect with local needs and realities (Drabek 1987; Qaurantelli 1989). As the floundering of the civil defense offices illustrated, many emergency management functions require buy-in and cooperation with emergent groups, civilians, and non-professionals. Caplow et al. argue such buy-in is best achieved with "persuasion rather than coercion" (1984, 20). The bureaucratic model is poorly equipped to convey critical situational awareness during the response phase (Waugh and Streib 2006). Furthermore, the ad hoc nature of response to major events, with their major uncertainties and conflicting demands, compel flexibility and adaptability in a system. Outside of the response phase, an imposed from the top-down template approach to mitigation and preparedness is ill-fitting and clunky for managing hazards that are particular to locales (Drabek 1987). The top-down model is also unable to account for specific social conditions that generate risk and influence capability for adaptation (Blaikie et al. 1992; Cutter et al. 2003).

The bureaucratic model is flawed not only when judged according to the outcome record, but also when viewed according to the legitimacy of its operating principles. Procedural justice concerns the fair application of procedures and rules when making decisions or managing conflicts (Lind and Tyler 1988; Tomlinson 2015). "Recognition, participation, and distribution of power" (Paavola 2006, 4) and inclusion of the vulnerable in decisions of governance (Boothby and Ager 2010) are established principals of procedural justice when making adaptations to environmental disruptions. With authority and decision-making centralized and distant, the bureaucratic model is poorly suited to achieve principles of procedural social justice (Loebach and Stewart 2016). And certain tendencies of the model in operations, including dictating policies, hoarding information and demanding compliance, are in direct opposition to principles of procedural justice (Neal and Philips 1995).

Disaster scholars of the late twentieth century offered a common set of policy recommendations to correct flaws in a system operating according to the bureaucratic model. In separate comparative analyses of local emergency management agencies, Quarantelli and Drabek concluded that key to successful management of emergencies is coordination and cooperation across organizations and with local groups. Critical in this system is a local manager who would "Seek to coordinate, not control" (Drabek 1986, 239). Drabek, Dynes, Quarantelli and others argue that disasters are fundamentally local events, and this implies that they are most effective and most equitable when managed locally and with community involvement (Quarantelli 1985; Wilson and Oyola-Yemaiel 2001). The International City Managers Assocation offered a set of recommendations aimed at improving a system at a crossroads (1981). They included specific organizational and structural features, including a local emergency manager, a local executive approval board, and a local emergency management organization engaged in routine organizational activities. In addition, ICMA advocated for a shift in strategies toward citizen involvement, commitment to public information sharing, and coordination across a diverse set of incorporated players.

The creation of the Federal Emergency Management Agency (FEMA) in 1979 involved consolidation of numerous agencies housed in separate departments and with fundamentally different missions and organizational philosophies. Its infant years were fraught with incoherence and disconnection. In 1993, following a widely publicized poor performance in responding to Hurricane Andrew, the National Academy of Public Administration wrote, "FEMA is like a patient in triage. The President and Congress must decide whether to treat it or let it die." In 1993, James Lee Witt, a former state director of emergency management, took the position of director and instituted sweeping reforms inside and outside the agency. Hailed as "The Witt Revolution," Witt ushered in a new system of disaster management that revolved around new goals and strategies, many of which were in line with the prescriptions of disaster scholarship up to the time. Themes in FEMA's new vision statement included "community plans, prepared in advance," "an informed public," and "communities built to withstand hazards" (FEMA 1997). Mitigation performed at and tailored to the local level became a new focus of disaster management, with *Project Impact: Building Disaster-Resistant Communities*, FEMA's centerpiece initiative launched tothis end. Under *Project Impact*, communities were encouraged to develop a community risk plan and to form *Disaster Resistant Community Planning Committee* "composed of local officials, business professionals, and other stakeholders with a shared interest in and obligation to protection the safety and economic stability of your community for the future" (FEMA 1997, 2). As opposed to top-down programs that impose rules and regulations on communities, under *Project Impact* FEMA provided mainly guidance and limited seed funding. While many of the shifts in strategies and policies survived Witt's tenure at FEMA, *Project Impac*t was short-lived; following the re-focusing event of 9/11 (Rubin 2012), a new presidential administration focused on shoreing up national security risks discontinued *Project Impact*. Nevertheless, there are partnerships and programs across the country that were established under *Project Impact* that persist (Hodeman and Patton 2008; Tierney 2012).

A shift in occurred following 9/11, when FEMA became subsumed under the Department of Homeland Security (DHS). In an effort to reorganize response under a more cohesive framework, DHS implemented The National Response Plan (NRP). Top management crafted the NRP, with little to no input from state and local emergency managers. A top-down system based on uniformity, and subordinate compliance through coercion and inducements returned (Birkland 2009). DHS centralized decision-making processes, reduced transparency, and discouraged collaboration and situational flexibility and adaptation (Tonsend 2006). Numerous leading disasters scholars, including Kathleen Tierney, William Waugh, Thomas Drabek, among others, declared these changes severe regressions back to a system of command and control, with implications for reduced local authority and loss of coordination with critical partners (Tierney 2006; Waugh and Streib 2006). Hurricane Katrina played, tragically, to all these tendencies. Even the White House itself concluded that a major hurdle in delivering relief in the Hurricane Katrina case was nongovernmental responders being unintegrated with public operations (White House 2006).

Systemic changes occurred again in 2008 when the National Response Framework (NRF) supplanted a flawed NRP. In its implementing document, the Department of Homeland Secuirty acknowledged the system as it stood was "bureaucratic and internally repetitive" (DHS 2008, 3), and that an effective system requires communities, NGO's and and all levels of governance to "complement each other in achieving shared goals" (2008, 4). FEMA administrator from 2009 to 2016, Craig Fulgate, described a need for a system integrated with communities and other involved actors, saying "a government-centric approach to disaster management will not be enough to meet the challenges posed by a catastrophic incident. That is why we must fully engage our entire social capacity" (Fugate 2011). FEMA adopted a set of principles and themes that revolved around improved community integration in 2011 under the title The Whole Community Approach. Central principles of Whole Community included "understand and meet the actual needs of the whole community; engage and empower all parts of the community; strengthen what works well in communities on a daily basis; recognize community capabilities and needs; foster relationships with community leaders; build and maintain partnerships; empower local action" (FEMA 2011).

Although Whole Community does signal a philosophical shift in the national emergency management system, new principles in the language of federal guidance documents has not been accompanied by policy changes that actually shift roles and responsibilities formally. The horizontal relationships undergirded by shared responsibility and common goals across a range of actors that is suggested by Whole Community is not represented in the statutory framework of disaster operations: The National Incident Management System (NIMS). From its national implementation under the NRP in 2004—and continuing to the present—NIMS and its element, the Incident Command System (ICS), provides the framework in which a range of organizations and actors, horizontally and vertically divided, are to "work together effectively and efficiently to prevent, prepare for, respond to, and recover from domestic incidents regardless of cause, size, or complexity" (DHS 2004, 1). It is praised by many for providing a template according to which roles, objectives and responsibility may be delineated in critical times and circumstances in which disparate agencies and organizations are involved and must collaborate and be unified in their efforts. But detractors argue that it is based on centralized leadership, hierarchical lines of authority and principles of command and control (Haddow and Bullock 2003; Kapucu and Garayev 2014; Jensen 2014; Jensen and Waugh 2014; Sevison 2014; Rubin 2007). It has been argued that in order for the vision of Whole Community to be fully realized there must be fundamental shifts at the level of governance structures and fiscal responsibilities (Crabo 2014; Rademacher 2014).

THE MISSING LINK

Over the last half a century, disaster scholarship has performed rigorous and trenchant evaluation and analyses of the effectiveness of legislation, policies, plans, and procedures related to hazards and disasters in the United States. Scholarship in this tradition has been extraordinarily impactful on policy. Notably, in this literature there has been a dominance of language and epistemological perspective from the field of public administration and with emphasis on patterns of institutional, group, and individual response—despite many of the foundational scholars having backgrounds in sociology (McEntire et al. 2002; Tierney 2007). In 2012, Kathleen Tierney reiterated the need for theoretical advancement in the field of disaster studies and made a specific call for research on governance that employs "a more inclusive approach that takes into account the broader societal contexts that influence disaster management, a wider array of institutional actors, and diverse mechanisms for encouraging collective action around disaster-related concerns " (2012, 358).

We suggest that there are gains to be made by placing decades of scholarship on disaster governance in an epistemological framework that incorporates theoretical concepts from a sociological literature on state–society relations. The sociological literature on state–society relations—and its explanations of development and democratization—instructs that successful cases feature certain qualities, values, and actions from the state and from citizens. Linking capital connects those two levels, creating a system where there once was only parts. Because concepts—by definition—are abstract, they move our thinking to a more analytical level. Ideally, those answers carry across cases because useful theory provides a kind of cognitive map that tells us where we have been and where we might go. We argue that linking capital is a critical element in that map, identifying key relationships—and the quality of those relationships—that can transform the social landscape.

As scholarship and some policy makers have noted, mitigation requires implementation at the community, group, and even individual level. But these decisions are never made in a power vacuum. Status linked to race, ethnicity, class, and gender shape designations of which people are worthy of aid and which people are not. Neither aid recipients nor organizational gatekeepers are immune to these influences and they fundamentally shape outcomes. Progressive practices, such as retro-fitting homes structures or even home relocation, requires time and expense from community members, even if knowhow and technological expertise comes from distant subject matter experts. Achieving compliance through coercion in the form of fines or withholding resources in event of losses, is a poor tool for developing trustful relationships—especially if requests made are ill-fitting to local needs and realities. Because disaster management is a continuous cycle, one must consider the future implications of achieving begrudging compliance through coercion. Compliance implies a power differential and is the opposite of the relationships that comprise linking capital. Instead of one side compelling or convincing the other, an ideal arrangement would feature different parties coming together around a set of agreed-upon values and shared norms. Forced compliance at one stage and at one time has implications that bleed into later stages and following cycles. Linking social capital provides a framework for conceptualize relations across divisions of authority and possession of resources as applied to hazard management, where past actions have bearing on future resilience.

Like so many elements of disaster management, it is in the response phase where the results of long-standing problems manifest. Many disaster response functions require shared goals and mutual trust. Poorly orchestrated and failed evacuations, for example, have been the result of community members not believing in the legitimacy of evacuation orders. Likewise, authorities' assumptions of groups' ability to evacuate and their lack of understanding of the barriers faced by vulnerable populations have contributed to the problem. Successful fulfillment of the function of evacuation depends on quality of relationship, and linking capital gives us a conceptual map for understanding capacity as related to quality of relationship. We suggest that linking capital can develop understanding of civilians and private organizations potential role in response. Emergent groups' ability to fill many holes in response is now well known (Drabek and McEntire 2003). It is also well-known that citizen involvement in response can cause many problems—especially given that so much public understanding of disasters consists of erroneous myths, often created and perpetuated by the media (Quarantelli 1985). That is why collaboration with emergent civil society responders is critical. What brings about such collaboration? We suggest that harnessing the best potential of emergent groups is achievable when there are long-standing community relationships across government systems and communities and undergirded by homologous values—in short, when there is linking capital.

We argue that the concept of linking capital is useful for lending new perspective on the history of disaster management in the United States. It can be seen that since the maligned civil defense years, there has been a decades long—but uneven—movement toward instituting community engagement in disaster management (Drabek 1987; Qaurantelli 1985; Rubin 2007). We argue that this evolution, driven by failures that made the need for community embeddedness and local level integration incontrovertible, consists of changes in institutional relationships aimed at generating linking social capital (Rubin 2016). An effort to achieve the central qualities of linking capital—embeddedness, reciprocal norms, homologous values, shared identity—can be heard in the language of organizational strategies taken by FEMA and organizational leaders in recent years: "shared goals," "empower local action," "foster local action." The progression has certainly not be continuous, nor is it complete. FEMA becoming subsumed under the DHS after 9/11 was a serious regression in this area—one that Hurricane Katrina, tragically, made glaringly visible.

Breaking linking capital down to its components allows us to look for the mechanisms that generate solidarity and a shared identity; it urges us to better understand the process of developing reciprocal norms. It advises us to explore the balance between sanctions and rewards and its role in creating enforceable trust. And it asks us to delineate how individually held values become collective values. One of these factors alone is not sufficient, because all are necessary. And in this way, the fates of the federal administrators and local actors become integrated, helping them to form a type of solidarity that is the basis for a shared identity. This is a tall order, to be sure, but complex problems such as how best to prevent, respond to and recover from disaster require complex solutions.

Framing disaster governance around linking capital and state–society relations opens up a new set of questions with important implications. We suggest a continuum exists in the extent to which institutions foster collaborations that bolster linking social capital, ranging from centralized, military intensive emergency management systems, to ones embedded deeply in an engaged citizenry. Despite systemic changes that encourage the development of linking social capital for disaster management, linking social capital appears highly variable across the United States and its territories. The contrasted responses between Hurricane Maria in Puerto Rico and Hurricane Irma in the state of Florida, with its famously developed disaster capacities, is a study in contrasts. We suggest that there is a need to interrogate the relations that undergird these different responses, which occurred in the same country within days of each other. One important distinction between these two cases, of course, is the dominant perception in society that some groups are "deserving" citizens and some are not. This speaks directly to the question of values—one of the key dimensions of linking social capital. In the second case, there were shared values between recipients and providers of assistance. Undoubtedly, this shared value grew out of a shared identity in a narrow vision of U.S. citizenship. In the first case, recipient values and aid provider values were misaligned, with the more powerful group withholding comprehensive aid due to a chasm around identity and belonging. In this way, applying a linking social capital framework helps differentiate successful response efforts from disastrous ones. Insofar as this is true in the U.S. case, we suspect it is also relevant to non-U.S. cases. We echo the recommendation of Quarantelli (1989), and more rencently McEntire (2012) and Drabek (2007), that there is a need for more studies of emergency management systems in other countries with different state–society relations.

Finally, we turn to the role of the emergency manager in the United States, recognized by scholars and government administrators alike as the actor whose profession is to align the goals of communities and higher-level actors. To what degree are local emergency managers embedded in their communities? Do they represent their communities in terms of classic social divides (race/ethnicity, gender, social class)? Do they possess sufficient autonomy, or are they vulnerable to elite capture? Are they the decision makers in times of extreme stress, or is their authority undermined by higher-level authorities and actors? These are pressing questions and we suggest that the theoretical perspective of linking capital provides a conceptual map to guide a search for these answers.

NOTES

1. According to a search utilizing the search term "social capital" in Scopus, 17,114 articles were published between 1968 and 2019 in social science journals (Search conducted January 11, 2019).

2. For example, in a search utilizing the search term "linking capital" in Scopus, we identified seventy-four articles published in social science journals. The majority of these were published in the past five years (Search conducted January 18, 2019).

REFERENCES

Abers, Rebecca. "From clientelism to cooperation: Local government, participatory policy, and civic organizing in Porto Alegre, Brazil." *Politics & Society* 26, 4 (1998): 511–537.

Abers, Rebecca. *Inventing Local Democracy: Grassroots Politics in Brazil.* Boulder: Lynne Rienner, 2000.

Aldrich, Daniel P. "The power of people: Social capital's role in recovery from the 1995 Kobe earthquake." *Natural Hazards* 56, 3 (2011): 595–611.

Baiocchi, Gianpaolo. *Militants and Citizens: The Politics of Participatory Democracy in Porto Alegre.* Stanford: Stanford University Press, 2005.

Bebbington, Anthony. "Capitals and capabilities: A framework for analyzing peasant viability, rural livelihoods and poverty." *World Development* 27, 12 (1999): 2021–2044.

Berenschot, Ward. "Everyday mediation: The politics of public service delivery in Gujarat, India." *Development and Change* 41, 5 (2010): 883–905.

Birkland, Thomas A. "Disasters, catastrophes, and policy failure in the homeland security era 1." *Review of Policy Research* 26, 4 (2009): 423–438.

Blaikie, Piers, Terry Cannon, Ian Davis, and Ben Wisner. *At Risk: Natural Hazards, People's Vulnerability, and Disasters.* New York: Routledge, 1994.

Boothby, Neil, and Alistair Ager. "Promoting a protective environment for children affected by disaster and war." In *A Child's Right to a Healthy Environment*, edited by James Garbarino and Garry Sigman, 105–121. New York: Springer, 2010.

Bourdieu, Pierre. "The forms of capital." In *Handbook of Theory and Research for the Sociology of Education*, edited by John Richardson, 241–258. New York: Greenwood, 1985.

Bourgois, Philippe. *In Search of Respect: Selling Crack in El Barrio.* Cambridge: Cambridge University Press, 1995.

Boyer, Evelyn F., and Wilbur J. Cohen. "Federal civil defense act of 1950: Summary and legislative history." *Social Security Bulletin* 14 (1951): 11.

Browning, Christopher R., Tama Leventhal, and Jeanne Brooks-Gunn. "Sexual initiation in early adolescence: The nexus of parental and community control." *American Sociological Review* 70, 5 (2005): 758–778.

Buckland, Jerry, and Matiur Rahman. "Community-based disaster management during the 1997 Red River Flood in Canada." *Disasters* 23, 2 (1999): 174–191.

Candland, Christopher. "Faith as social capital: Religion and community development in southern Asia." *Policy Sciences* 33 (2000): 355–374.

Cannon, Terry. "Vulnerability analysis and the explanation of 'natural' disasters." In *Disasters, Development and Environment*, edited by Ann Varley, 13–29. Chichester: John Wiley and Sons, 1994.

Caplow, T., H. M. Bahr, and B. A. Chadwick. *Analysis of the Readiness of Local Communities for Integrated Emergency Management Planning (No. 183–186)*. Charlottesville, VA: United Research Services, 1984.

Carbill, Amy, and Yvonne Rademacher. "Whole community: Local, state, and federal relationships: A practitioner's perspective." In *Critical Issues in Disaster Science and Management*, edited by Joseph Trainor and Tony Subbio, 9–52. Emmitsburg, MD: FEMA, 2014.

Chamlee-Wright, Emily, and Virgil Henry Storr. "There's no place like New Orleans: Sense of place and community recovery in the Ninth Ward after Hurricane Katrina." *Journal of Urban Affairs* 31, 5 (2009): 615–634.

Cleaver, Frances. "The inequality of social capital and the reproduction of chronic poverty." *World Development* 33, 6 (2005): 893–906.

Coleman, James S. *Foundations of Social Theory*. Cambridge: Harvard University Press, 1990.

Collier, Paul. "Social capital and poverty." The World Bank social capital initiative, Working Paper No. 4. Washington, DC: The World Bank, 1998.

Collier, Ruth B., and David Collier. *Shaping the Political Arena: Critical Junctures, the Labor Movement, and Regime Dynamics in Latin America*. Princeton: Princeton University Press, 1991.

Cox, Robin S., and Karen-Marie Elah Perry. "Like a fish out of water: Reconsidering disaster recovery and the role of place and social capital in community disaster resilience." *American Journal of Community Psychology* 48, 3–4 (2011): 395–411.

Crane, Jonathan. "The epidemic theory of ghettos and neighbor-hood effects on dropping out and teenage childbearing." *American Journal of Sociology* 96, 5 (1991): 1226–1259.

Cutter, Susan L., Bryan J. Boruff, and W. Lynn Shirley. "Social vulnerability to environmental hazards." *Social Science Quarterly* 84, 2 (2003): 242–261.

Das Gupta, Monica, Helene Grandvoinnet, and Mattia Romani. "State-community synergies in community-driven development." *The Journal of Development Studies* 40, 3 (2004): 27–58.

Dauber, Michele Landis. *The Sympathetic State: Disaster Relief and the Origins of the American Welfare State*. Chicago: University of Chicago Press, 2013.

Department of Homeland Security. *National Incident Management System*. Washington, DC: DHS, 2004.

Department of Homeland Security. *National Response Framework*. Washington, DC: DHS, 2008.

Drabek, Thomas E. *Human System Responses to Disaster: An Inventory of Sociological Findings*. New York: Springer-Verlag, 1986.

Drabek, Thomas E. "Understanding disaster warning responses." *The Social Science Journal* 36, 3 (1999): 515–523.

Drabek, Thomas E., and David A. McEntire. "Emergent phenomena and the sociology of disaster: Lessons, trends and opportunities from the research literature." *Disaster Prevention and Management* 12, 2 (2003): 97–112.

Dynes, Russel R. *Organized Behavior in Disasters*. Disaster Research Center. Monograph. Serial No. 3. Columbus: Ohio State University, 1974.

Dynes, Russel R. "Community emergency planning: False assumptions and inappropriate analogies." *International Journal of Mass Emergencies and Disasters* 12, 2 (1994): 141–158.

Dynes, Russel R. "Social capital: Dealing with community emergencies." *Homeland Security Affairs* 2 (2006): 1–26.

Edwards, Rosalind, Jane Franklin, and Janet Holland. *Families and Social Capital: Exploring the Issues*. Families and Social Capital Research Group, Working Paper No. 1. London: South Bank University, 2003.

Elliott, James R., Timothy J. Haney, and Petrice Sams-Abiodun. "Limits to social capital: Comparing network assistance in two New Orleans neighborhoods devastated by Hurricane Katrina." *The Sociological Quarterly* 51, 4 (2010): 624–648.

Emirbayer, Mustafa, and Jeff Goodwin. "Network analysis, culture & the problem of agency." *American Journal of Sociology* 99, 6 (1994): 1411–1454.

Etzioni, Amitai. "Positive aspects of community and the dangers of fragmentation." *Development and Change* 27, 2 (1996): 301–314.

Evans, Peter. *Embedded Autonomy: States and Industrial Transformation*. Princeton: Princeton University Press, 1995.

Evans, Peter. "Government action, social capital and development: Reviewing the evidence on synergy." *World Development* 24, 6 (1996): 1119–1132.

Fafchamps, Marcel. "Development and social capital." *Journal of Development Studies* 42, 7 (2007): 1180–1198.

Federal Emergency Management Administration. *Strategic Plan: Partnership for a Safer Future* (Section: Where We Plan to Go). Washington, DC: FEMA, 1997.

Federal Emergency Management Agency. *Project Impact: Building a Disaster Resistant Community*. Washington, DC: FEMA, 1997.

Fine, Ben. *Social Capital Versus Social Theory: Political Economy and Social Science at the Turn of the Millennium*. London: Routledge, 2001.

Fine, Ben. "They f**k you up those social capitalists." *Antipode: A Radical Journal of Geography* 34, 4 (2002): 796–799.

Fox, Jonathan A., and Lloyd D. Brown. *The Struggle for Accountability: The World Bank, NGOs, and Grassroots Movements*. Cambridge: MIT Press, 1998.

Fung, Archon, and Erik O. Wright. *Deepening Democracy: Institutional Innovations in Empowered Participatory Governance*. London: Verso, 2003.

Gittell, Ross, and Avis Vidal. *Community Organizing: Building Social Capital as a Development Strategy*. Thousand Oaks: Sage, 1998.

Granovetter, Mark. "The strength of weak ties." *American Journal of Sociology* 78, 6 (1973): 1360–1380.

Grootaert, Christiann. "Social capital: The missing link?" Social capital initiative Working Paper No. 3. Washington, DC: The World Bank, 1998.

Grootaert, Christian, and Narayan Deepa. "Local institutions, poverty and household welfare in Bolivia." *World Development* 32, 7 (2004): 1179–1198.

Guijt, Irene, and Meera K. Shah. "Waking up to power, conflict and process." In *The Myth of Community: Gender Issues in Participatory Development*, edited by Irene Guijt and Meera K. Shah, 1–24. London: Intermediate Technology Publications, 1998.

Heller, Patrick. "Social capital as a product of class mobilization and state intervention: Industrial workers in Kerala, India." *World Development* 24, 6 (1996): 1055–1071.

Heller, Patrick, and Isaac T. Thomas. "Democracy and development: Decentralized planning in Kerala." In *Deepening Democracy: Institutional Innovations in Empowered Participatory Governance*, edited by Archon Fund and Eric O. Wright, 77–110. London: Verso, 2003.

Holdeman, Eric, and Ann Patton. "Project impact initiative to create disaster-resistant communities demonstrates worth in Kansas years later." *Emergency Management* 2008. Retrieved September 22, 2020 from https://www.govtech.com/em/disaster/Project-Impact-Initiative-to.html

Hunt, Carter A., William H. Durham, and Claire M. Menke. "Social capital in development: Bonds, bridges, and links in OSA and Golfito, Costa Rica." *Human Organization* 74, 3 (2015): 217–229.

Jensen, J. "Reflections on NIMS: An academic perspective." In *Criticial Issues in Disaster Science and Management*, edited by Joseph Trainor and Tony Subbio, 223–282. Emmitsburg, MD: FEMA, 2014.

Jensen, Jessica, and Willim L. Waugh Jr. "The United States' experience with the incident command system: What we think we know and what we need to know more about." *Journal of Contingencies and Crisis Management* 22, 1 (2014): 5–17.

Kapucu, Naim, and Vener Garayev. "Structure and network performance: Horizontal and vertical networks in emergency management." *Administration & Society* 48, 8 (2016): 931–961.

Kelly, Linda, Patrick Kilby, and Nalini Kasynathan. "Impact measurement for NGOs: Experiences from India and Sri Lanka." *Development in Practice* 14, 5 (2004): 696–702.

King, Lawrence P., and Aleksandra Sznajder. "The state-led transition to liberal capitalism: Neoliberal, organizational, world-systems, and social structural explanations of Poland's economic success." *American Journal of Sociology* 112, 3 (2006): 751–801.

Klinenberg, Eric. "Review of a paradise built in hell: The extraordinary communities that arise in disaster." *Mother Jones* 34, Sept./Oct. (2009): 75.

Krishna, Anirudh. *Active Social Capital: Tracing the Roots of Development and Democracy.* New York: Columbia University Press, 2002.

Kumar, Sanjay, and Stuart Corbridge. "Programmed to fail? Development projects and the politics of participation." *Journal of Development Studies* 39, 2 (2002): 73–103.

Levitt, Peggy, and N. Rajaram. "Reform through return? Migration, health and development in Gujarat, India." *Migration Studies* 1, 3 (2013): 338–362.

Lin, Nan, Karen Cook, and Ronald S. Burt. *Social Capital: Theory and Research.* New York: Aldine de Gruyter, 2001.

Lind, Allen E., and Tom R. Tyler. *The Social Psychology of Procedural Justice.* New York: Plenum, 1988.

Loebach, Peter, and Julie Stewart. "Vital linkages: A study of the role of linking social capital in a Philippine disaster recovery and rebuilding effort." *Social Justice Research* 28, 3 (2015): 339–362.

Lofland, John, and Lyn H. Lofland. *Analyzing Social Settings: A Guide to Qualitative Observation and Analysis.* Belmont: Wadsworth Publishing Company, 1995.

McEntire, David A., Christopher Fuller, Chad W. Johnston, and Richard Weber. "A comparison of disaster paradigms: The search for a holistic policy guide." *Public Administration Review* 62, 3 (2002): 267–281.

Mimaki, Junko, and Rajib Shaw. "Enhancement of disaster preparedness with social capital and community capacity: A perspective from a comparative case study of rural communities in Kochi, Japan." *SUISUI Hydrological Research Letters* 1 (2007): 5–10.

Mondal, Abdul H. "Social capital formation: The role of NGO rural development programs in Bangladesh." *Policy Sciences* 33 (2000): 459–475.

Montiel, Cristina J. "Social psychological dimensions of political conflict resolution in the Philippines." *Journal of Peace Psychology* 1, 2 (1995): 149–159.

Moody, James, and Douglas R. White. "Structural cohesion and embeddedness: A hierarchical concept of social groups." *American Sociological Review* 68, 1 (2003): 103–127.

Moore, Spencer, Eugenia Eng, and Mark Daniel. "International NGOs and the role of network centrality in humanitarian aid operations: A case study of coordination curing the 2000 Mozambique floods." *Disasters* 27, 4 (2003): 305–318.

Nakagawa, Yuko, and Rajib Shaw. "Social capital: A missing link to disaster recovery." *International Journal of Mass Emergencies and Disasters* 22, 1 (2004): 5–34.

Narayan, Deepa. *Voices of the Poor.* New York: Oxford University Press, 2000.

Neal, David M., and Brenda D. Phillips. "Effective emergency management: Reconsidering the bureaucratic approach." *Disasters* 19, 4 (1995): 327.

Norris, Fran, Susan P. Stevens, Betty Pfefferbaum, Karen F. Wyche, and Rose L. Pfefferbaum. "Community resilience as a metaphor, theory, set of capacities, and strategy for disaster readiness." *American Journal of Community Psychology* 41, 1–2 (2008): 127–150.

Okten, Cagla, and Una Okonkwo Osili. "Social networks and credit access in Indonesia." *World Development* 32, 7 (2004): 1225–1246.

Osborne, Stephen P. *Public-Private Partnerships: Theory and Practice in International Perspective.* London: Routledge, 2000.

Paavola, Joan. "Justice in adaptation to climate change in Tanzania." In *Fairness in Adaptation to Climate Change*, edited by W. Neil Adger, 201–222. Cambridge: MIT Press, 2006.

Patrick, Kilby. "The strength of networks: The local NGO response to the tsunami in India." *Disasters* 32, 1 (2008): 120–130.

Paxton, Pamela. "Social capital and democracy: An interdependent relationship." *American Sociological Review* 67, 2 (2002): 254–277.

Pelling, Mark. "Participation, social capital and vulnerability to urban flooding in Guyana." *Journal of International Development* 10, 4 (1998): 469–486.

Pelling, Mark. "Learning from others: The scope and challenges for participatory disaster risk assessment." *Disasters* 31, 4 (2007): 373–385.

Pew Research Center Forum on Religion & Public Life. Global Christianity. 2011. http://features.pewforum.org/global-christianity/population-number.php. Accessed May 15, 2012.

Portes, Alejandro. "The social origins of the Cuban enclave economy of Miami." *Sociological Perspectives* 30, 4 (1987): 340–372.

Portes, Alejandro. "Social capital: Its origins and applications in modern sociology." *Annual Review of Sociology* 24 (1998): 1–24.

Portes, Alejandro, and Patricia Landolt. "Social capital: Promise and pitfalls of its role in development." *Journal of Latin American Studies* 32, 2 (2000): 529–547.

Putnam, Robert D. *Bowling Alone: The Collapse and Revival of American Community.* New York: Touchstone, 2000.

Putnam, Robert D., Robert Leonardi, and Raffaella Nanetti. *Making Democracy Work: Civic Traditions in Modern Italy.* Princeton: Princeton University Press, 1993.

Quarantelli, Enrico L. *Organizational Behavior in Disasters and Implications for Disaster Planning.* Emmitsburg, MD: FEMA, 1985.

Quarantelli, Enrico L. "Disaster crisis management: A summary of research findings." *Journal of Management Studies* 25, 4 (1988): 373–385.

Rademacher, Yvonne. "Whole community: Local, state, and federal relationships: An academic perspective." In *Critical Issues in Disaster Science and Management*, edited by Joseph E. Trainor and Tony Subbio, 9–52. Emmitsburg, MD: FEMA, 2014.

Ride, Anouk, and Diane Bretherton. *Community Resilience in Natural Disasters.* New York: Palgrave Macmillan, 2011.

Rubin, Claire B. *Emergency Management: The American Experience 1900–2010.* New York: Routledge, 2012.

Rubin, Olivier. "The political dimension of "linking social capital": Current analytical practices and the case for recalibration." *Theory and Society* 45, 5 (2016): 429–449.

Schafft, Kai A., and David L. Brown. "Social capital, social networks, and social power." *Social Epistemology* 17, 4 (2003): 329–342.

Schneider, Saundra K. "Governmental response to disasters: The conflict between bureaucratic procedures and emergent norms." *Public Administration Review* 52, 2 (1992): 135–145.

Sevison, Tim, and Jessica Jensen. "Reflections on NIMS." In *Critical Issues in Disaster Science and Management*, edited by Joseph E. Trainor and Tony Subbio, 223–282. Emmitsburg, MD: FEMA, 2014.

Sobelson, Robyn K., Corinne J. Wigington, Victoria Harp, and Bernice B. Bronson. "A whole community approach to emergency management: Strategies and best practices of seven community programs." *Journal of Emergency Management* 13, 4 (2015): 349.

Stack, Carol. *All Our Kin.* New York: Basic Books, 1974.

Szreter, Simon. "The state of social capital: Bringing back in power, politics, and history." *Theory and Society* 31, 5 (2002): 573–621.

Szreter, Simon, and Michael Woolcock. "Health by association? Social capital, social theory, and the political economy of public health." *International Journal of Epidemiology* 33, 4 (2004): 650–667.

Tierney, Kathleen. "From the margins to the mainstream? Disaster research at the crossroads." *Annual Review of Sociology* 33 (2007): 503–525.

Tierney, Kathleen. "Disaster governance: Social, political and economic dimensions." *Annual Review of Environment and Resources* 37 (2012): 341–363.

Tomlinson, Luke. "Getting a seat at the table: Fair participation in the UNFCCC." In *Procedural Justice in the United Nations Framework Convention on Climate Change*, edited by Luke Tomlinson, 85–107. Geneva: Springer, 2015.

Torres, Ariana P., Maria I. Marshall, and Sandra Sydnor. "Does social capital pay off? The case of small business resilience after Hurricane Katrina." *Journal of Contingencies and Crisis Management* 27, 2 (2018): 1–14.

Townsend, Frances Fargo. *The Federal Response to Hurricane Katrina: Lessons Learned*. Washington, DC: The White House, 2006.

Waldinger, Roger. "The 'other side' of embedded ness: A case-study of the interplay of economy and ethnicity." *Ethnic and Racial Studies* 18, 3 (2010): 550–580.

Waugh Jr, William L. "Mechanisms for collaboration in emergency management: ICS, NIMS, and the problem with command and control." In *The Collaborative Public Manager: New Ideas for the Twenty-First Century*, 157–175. Georgetown University Press, 2009.

Waugh Jr, William L., and Gregory Streib. "Collaboration and leadership for effective emergency management." *Public Administration Review* 66, S1 (2006): 131–140.

Wilson, Jennifer, and Arthur Oyola-Yemaiel. "The evolution of emergency management and the advancement towards a profession in the United States and Florida." *Safety Science* 39, 1–2 (2001): 117–131.

Woolcock, Michael. "Social capital and economic development: Toward a theoretical synthesis and policy framework." *Theory and Society* 27 (1998): 151–208.

Woolcock, Michael. "The place of social capital in understanding social and economic outcomes." *Canadian Journal of Policy Research* 2 (2001): 11–17.

Woolcock, Michael, and Deepa Narayan. "Social capital: Implications for development theory, research, and policy." *The World Bank Research Observer* 15, 1 (2000): 225–249.

Zhou, Min. "Revisiting ethnic entrepreneuership: convergences, controversies, and conceptual advancements." *International Migration Review* 38, 3 (2004): 1040–1074.

Zhou, Min, and Carl L. Bankston. "Social capital and the adaptation of the second generation: The case of Vietnamese youth in New Orleans." In *The New Second Generation*, edited by Alejandro Portes, 197–220. New York: Russell Sage Foundation, 1996.

Chapter 3

Working for the Clampdown

The Impact of Hyper-Decentralization on Voter Registration and Ballot Access in the Wake of Natural Disasters

Paul S. Adams

A system that deprives too many of its citizens of the right to register to vote and access the ballot cannot be easily classified as democracy. The United States exhibits many characteristics that lead to the questioning of its inclusion in the community of advanced liberal democracies. Criminal disenfranchisement, registration barriers, and hurdles to ballot access combine to create one of the most obstructive voting systems among its democratic peers. Registration and voting barriers disproportionately affect Americans already beset by social and economic inequality. Substantial data on disenfranchisement, registration obstacles, and voter suppression paint an unflattering portrait of significant, institutionalized voter inequality. Under normal circumstances, this is a significant flaw in American democracy and voter inclusion. However, when under stress from natural disasters, public health threats, and other extraordinary conditions, the levels of inequality in voter rights are magnified. Holding free, fair, and open elections and demonstrating the most critical procedures of democracy even under emergency conditions should be evidence of a strong, vibrant, responsive, and institutionalized democratic regime and a testament to the importance and priority of voting. Yet, the evidence from the past few decades suggests that natural disasters and other public emergencies have sometimes become opportunities for even more unequal treatment and increased effective disenfranchisement.

Future primary and general elections will likely be disrupted by the increasing incidence of natural disasters and public health threats. The existing American system of voter registration and polling is one that is highly decentralized to the state, county, and municipal levels. The lack of uniformity, equal application of voter and election law, and differentiated resources of state and local governments have led to significant barriers to registration and ballot access for many Americans. In the vast majority of cases, these Americans are those that already suffer from social and economic inequality. The state and municipal institutions that have been the source of existing registration and ballot access restrictions are in positions to magnify this inequality further in the wake of natural disasters. This chapter shall analyze the impact of decentralization on voter registration and ballot access and how natural disasters worsen disparities existent in the system. Disasters and other crises stress the already fragmented system, allowing not only increased ineffectiveness and non-conformity, but also providing opportunities for partisan and politically biased manipulation. This research argues that without significant federal and state-level policy responses, training, reporting requirements, and financial support, the prevalence of natural disaster induced voter suppression is likely to increase. However, even with federal and state action, the heavily fragmented system of American voter registration and polling place operations is prone to resist institutional centralization and uniformity. The very nature of disasters likely means even more variation and unequal treatment not only from state to state, within states, or even within counties and municipalities. This research contends that any long-term solutions to voter registration and ballot access suppression will be challenging even under non-emergency circumstances due to the extraordinary level of decentralization in the United States' electoral and voting systems.

This research argues that one of, if not perhaps the most critical, the primary causes of inequality in voter registration and ballot access is the decentralized nature of the American election system. This system devolves important legal and operational voting policies and practices to the states, counties, municipal governments, and even individual precinct officials. As will be detailed in latter sections of this chapter, this decentralization has beget a system in which there is a remarkable lack of uniformity and conformity to voting law. This makes the system susceptible to not only misinterpretation and misapplication of existing voting law but also one more easily manipulated by public officials, political parties, and other partisan actors to alter voter eligibility, registration, and ballot access. Natural disasters provide not only stresses to this system that are likely to increase errors in application of voting laws but also opportunities for greater political manipulation. This research concludes that public law, political science, and public policy researchers as well as policymakers at the local, state, and federal level must seriously consider implications of natural disasters as part of the study of and preparation for American elections in terms of equality of registration and ballot access. The impacts of recent hurricanes and the coronavirus pandemic of 2020 are illustrative of the negative impacts that natural disasters and public health emergencies can have on voting. The increasing incidence of natural disasters, and perhaps pandemics and other public health emergencies, will likely make this issue ever more salient in future election cycles. Yet even with federal and state action, the complexity and scale of standardizing registration and ballot access across the United States is daunting and likely to remain an increasingly stubborn concern.

ASSESSING WHAT WE KNOW ABOUT BARRIERS TO VOTER REGISTRATION AND BALLOT ACCESS

Americans beset by social and economic inequality are already subject to greater disenfranchisement and voter suppression that other segments of society. Through criminal disenfranchisement, high registration barriers, strict voter identification laws, changing and limiting polling places, long waiting lines to vote, and other phenomena, minority and lower income voters are disproportionately and increasingly the victims of policies, procedures, and institutions of the American system of voter registration and ballot access. Even under normal circumstances, the patterns of formal and informal disenfranchisement are a serious problem of American democracy. Natural disasters and their aftermath illuminate and further magnify these conditions. There is substantial literature and social science research on the existing biases and gaps in voter registration and ballot access correlating to race, ethnicity, class, education, and other demographic features of American citizens. This section shall briefly summarize some of the major sources and impacts of inequality in voter registration and ballot access in the United States. Specifically, this research is focused upon the institutions, policies, and procedures that are not only likely to explain inequality in registration and ballot access in normal times but also those most susceptible in times of natural disaster.

Lower voter registration and turnout among economically disadvantaged and ethnic minority populations are explained from both sociological and institutional approaches. The sociological argument tends to suggest that voter registration and voting itself are learned behaviors that tend to be emulated upon parental or peer modeling. There is sizeable evidence that registering to vote, party affiliation, and actual casting of ballots are strongly correlated to familial, community, and peer behavior (Verba et al. 2005; Plutzer 2002; Xu 2005). This evidence could suggest that lower registration and turnout among economically disadvantaged and minority citizens is explained without regard to institutional barriers. However, that would presuppose that institutional barriers are not possible root causes of familial, community, and peer non-registration and non-voting. In many ways, this does create a chicken and egg dilemma in that sociological variables may explain continuing non-registration and non-voting but are perhaps initially due to institutional variables that generationally beget non-participation. This research does not seek to answer this conundrum, rather it does consider the complexity and uncertainty of clearly identifying the sources of non-registration and non-voting among disadvantaged social groups. The primary argument in this chapter is that institutional barriers are a significant and important causal mechanism in the suppression of disadvantaged citizens and become magnified during times of natural disaster and crisis.

Voter Registration

Registering to vote has become significantly easier in the past three decades yet registration gaps between economically disadvantaged and advantaged citizens remains high. Recent studies illustrate that lower socioeconomic status and non-white ethnicity continue to be associated with lower levels of voter registration and turnout. Bhatt, Dechter, and Holden correlate the relationship between levels of income and education with both lower registration and turnout in elections between 1996 and 2012 (2020). One of the major barriers typically correlated to voter registration has been the "costs" of the registration process (Cloward and Piven 1989; Piven and Cloward 2000). In this context, costs are the informational and procedural effort needed to properly obtain, complete, and submit a successful voter registration application. Prior to the 1990s, the costs associated with voter registration varied significantly from state to state and even within states. Obtaining the form, completing the application with required information, and remitting the form to local election authorities may not seem like a significant barrier, yet lack of coherent and useful information of the registration requirements and process have often provided a meaningful hurdle to registration for some Americans. States with more stringent registration laws and procedures tend to have more of an impact on poorer and less educated citizens while states with more accessible and easy registration procedures see greater such registration numbers (Jackson et al. 1998; Brown et al. 1999; Avery and Peffeley 2005).

Efforts to lower informational and procedural costs of registration such as the National Voter Registration Act of 1993 (often known as the Motor Voter Act) have shown some impacts on registration of minorities and those from disadvantaged socioeconomic backgrounds (Rugeley and Jackson 2009; Wolfinger and Hoffman 2001). However, even with NVRA and other efforts to reduce the informational and procedural costs of registration, there is still a significant gap between minorities and whites. Wolfinger and Hoffman demonstrated that African-Americans and Latinos were less likely to utilize the NVRA than whites and that those with less education were also less likely to use such registration opportunities (2001). Even when afforded an opportunity in public assistance offices or driver licensing centers, fewer minorities opted for registration (Wolfinger and Hoffman 2001). Some studies have conversely shown that when provided registration and voting information in "low-cost" manners, those from lower income and education groups do register at higher numbers. In-person and mailed registration drives in poorer areas, where information is increased and costs are decreased, do result in higher registration and turnout in some cases (Nickerson 2015). This suggests that lower costs in time and effort and greater information do provide incentives for registration (Bhatt et al. 2020) Nonetheless, overall registration and turnout for minorities and economically disadvantaged citizens is typically still much lower than those of whites and more economically advantaged citizens. Automatic registration, motor voter, and online voter registration in some states have combined to dramatically lower the costs of registration. Despite these significant advances, gaps remain. Some research has suggested that levels of education and class have limited impact on the ability to register to vote and other variables, likely sociological, must be at play (Wattenberg 2002; Nagler 1991).

While accessing, completing, and submitting voter registrations is easier than in the past, this does not mean that voter registrations are universally accepted and processed by local election officials. One of the possible barriers in voter registration by minorities, economically disadvantaged, and other specific groups of citizens is the rejection of voter registration applications by local election officials. Most rejections are based on incomplete or improper completion of the voter registration form, illegibility, or determinations of ineligibility by local election officials at the county and municipal level. Nonetheless, the disposition of rejections does appear to have biases and may be based on flawed, improper, or biased interpretations of state laws. There is increasing evidence that rejection of voter registration applications of minority and economically disadvantaged citizens is much higher than of white and more economically advantaged ones (Merivaki and Smith 2020; Merivaki 2019, 2020, 2020a). While minorities are most impacted, the homeless, college students, rural residents, and others may see higher than average rejections of voter registration applications (Hanrahan 1994; Ruth et al. 2007; MacDonald and Hamner 2019). This is sometimes associated with the lack of an acceptable local address or use of addresses that do not conform to known residential locations. For college students, local election officials may also reject such applications based on flawed interpretation and administration of state law regarding the ability of students to register and vote using their college addresses (MacDonald and Hamner 2019).

Once on the voter rolls, a registered voter may not necessarily stay on the roll. The purging of names from voter rolls is a controversial and nonuniform practice. States have differential rules for purging names from the voter lists for a wide range of issues including nonvoting, change of residence, criminal disenfranchisement, and other rationale. So once registered, there are numerous ways that a voter could be purged from the rolls. There is a growing body of evidence about the unequal and non-uniform use of voter roll purges (Brater 2018; Merivaki 2020). Brater, authoring a 2018 report from the Brennan Center for Justice, cites numerous instances of improper and mismanaged voter purges from across the United States over the past decade. Most such cases has a disproportionate impact in minority and low-income communities (Brater 2018). Merikavi's research on voter purges in Mississippi show some of the major pitfalls and biases of the process. Criminal disenfranchisement is one of the most notable and contentious reasons for being purged from the rolls. The extensive literature on criminal disenfranchisement cannot be fully explored in this chapter for obvious reasons. Importantly, criminal disenfranchisement has been conclusively shown to disproportionately impact minorities and economically disadvantaged citizens. Purging the voting rolls, no matter the rationale, has decisively stronger impacts low-income and minority communities.

Voter registration issues and barriers ranging from the costs and procedures of registration, rejection of registrations, and purging of voters all demonstrate many shared characteristics. First, the results of registration barriers have a disproportionate impact on minority and low-income voters. Criminal disenfranchisement might be the most highlighted and contentious form of voter discrimination, but other barriers to registration, purging the rolls, and registration rejections all share the same class and ethnic biases. The second shared characteristic is the role of state and local election offices and officials in implementing, enforcing, and institutionalizing these barriers. As will be discussed later and is critical to this research, voter registration barriers are products of state and local laws, policies, and practices that create and sustain such inequality. While registration barriers are important and influential in suppressing the vote of many economically disadvantaged and minority citizens, even those that get on and stay on the voter rolls may face significant obstacles to casting their ballots on election day.

Ballot Access

The data on lower voter turnout by minority and economically disadvantaged citizens in voluminous. The preponderance of evidence shows that minorities and economically disadvantaged citizens vote at a lower rate than white and more economically advantaged citizens (Piven and Cloward 1989; Leighley and Nagler 1992; Verba et al. 1978; Avery and Peffley 2005; Franko et al. 2016). This research will not rehash this evidence and accepts that even once registered, there is significantly and consistently lower turnout among minorities and economically disadvantaged citizens in the United States. The critical questions related to this research are those that pertain to voters who, once registered and seeking the opportunity to vote, fail to gain access to the ballot.

One of the most contentious and debated issues in recent years has been that of the potential impact of voter identification laws on minority turnout. The literature on this particular issue is nearly as voluminous as that on criminal disenfranchisement. Those that argue that voter identification laws are likely to suppress the turnout of minority and economically disadvantaged citizens point to several key issues. Voter identification laws increase the costs of voting in that whites are far more likely to possess valid forms of identification than minorities (Highton 2017; Barreto et al. 2019). Voter identification laws increase the costs of registration and voting and hence disproportionately impact less economically advantaged and educated voters. Even if costs are actually low, those from lower socioeconomic backgrounds are more likely to see such barriers as significant and preclude their registration and turnout. The bulk of the research suggests that voter identification laws are obstacles and do suppress minority voting (Barreto et al. 2019; Hajnal et al. 2017, 2018). That being said, there is significant literature that argues the impact is far smaller and less consistent and important than is normally argued (Erikson and Minnite 2009; Grimmer et al. 2018; Hood and Bullock 2012; Hood and Buchanan 2020).

Rather than go down the rabbit hole into this debate, this research argues that while the impact of voter identification may or may not have significant impacts on minority and economically disadvantaged voter turnout, the existence of strict voter identification laws and the perception of many voters could themselves have impacts on participation. Access to valid types of identification do appear to be more inconsistent among minorities and the economically disadvantaged (Barreto et al. 2019). Expiration and loss of identification are more likely to impact minority or low-income voters than whites and economically advantaged voters that possess multiple types of valid identification (driver's licenses, passports, government identification cards, etc.) or can easily afford to quickly replace lost or expired identification cards.

Importantly, the voter identification requirement is one that is heavily decentralized to and dependent upon state law. Enforcement of identification laws is even more fragmented to the county and precinct levels. Recognition and acceptance of acceptable identification, while often defined under state law, may lack uniform enforcement at the county, municipal, and precinct levels. Overall, voter identification impacts on turnout may be disputed, but they do appear to have sizeable impacts on minority and disadvantaged participation and reflect the importance of state laws and local election administration and procedures in creating an environment that is unwelcoming for many minority and low-income citizens.

While voter identification requirements add procedural costs and uncertainty to the voting experience of many minority and economically disadvantaged Americans, perhaps no phenomena has become more emblematic of increased costs and uncertainty in voting than extraordinarily long lines and wait times for many voters. In 2012, 1 in 10 voters waited more than 30 minutes to cast a ballot while 3.5 million voters waited in excess of one hour (Pettigrew 2017). The Bipartisan Policy Center estimates that more than half a million voters failed to vote in 2016 due to polling place management issues and long lines (Weil et al. 2019). A report from the Brennan Center for Justice estimates that in 2018, approximately three million voters waited 30 minutes or more to vote in the November general election. Wait times of over five hours have become far more commonplace in many elections over the past decade (Pettigrew 2017; Klain et al. 2020). In 2020 primaries, long lines with wait times in excess of two hours were commonplace in Georgia, Wisconsin, Kentucky, California, Texas, Arizona, and elsewhere. Long wait times are inconvenient and may ultimately drive voters away from the current and subsequent elections (Pettigrew 2017; Klain et al. 2020).

Black and Latino Americans face longer wait times than white voters (Pettigrew 2017; Klain et al. 2020; Harris 2020; Graham 2013). Minorities are six times more likely to wait more than an hour to vote than whites (Pettigrew 2017). Pettigrew further demonstrates that this "racial" gap is not just exhibited at the national level but even in precincts in the same county, town, or even neighborhood (2017). Creating long lines is one way to create effective disenfranchisement of voters and the growing evidence from the last decade indicates that this problem is much larger in minority and economically disadvantaged communities (Pettigrew 2017; Klain et al. 2020; Vasilogambros 2018; Harris 2020). If long lines affected all voters systematically the problem would be one of just inconvenience or mismanagement, but when the impact is disproportionately afflicting only certain groups of voters, the political, social, and ethnic consequences are different (Pettigrew 2017). When costs are lower, those from disadvantaged socioeconomic backgrounds are more likely to engage in the voting process, long lines and waiting times have the opposite effect (Bhatt et al. 2020).

The causes of long lines and wait times are multivariate. Increased turnout is one obvious culprit as voter turnout has increased since the 1990s especially in presidential and midterm elections such as in 2008, 2010, 2012, 2016, and 2018. However, the long waits and lines are not proportional to the increased turnout. Longer ballots with more races and ballot questions can also increase wait times. Yet analysis of wait times usually takes this into account (Pettigrew 2017). The closure of polling places has been one of the most notable trends over the past decade. After the Supreme Court struck down parts of the Voting Rights Act, the closure of hundreds of polling places across southern, Midwestern, and western states has resulted. In 2018, Georgia closed numerous polling locations in ten counties with large African-American populations (Vasilogambros 2018). Reductions of polling places in Georgia, Florida, North Carolina, Alabama, Texas, Louisiana, Indiana, and Arizona all seemed to be geared toward communities with large minority populations (Vasilogambros 2018; Harris 2020).

The drivers of polling place consolidation and closure are often partisan but can also be budgetary. In more rural and mixed counties, consolidation of polling places due to declining populations and fewer poll workers can have similar effects on older, rural, and economically disadvantaged whites. Barton County, Kansas reduced polling places from 40 to 11 over the past few decades significantly increasing the distance for many to vote (Vasilogambros 2018). In Maricopa County, Arizona in 2016, polling locations were reduced by 70%, from 200 to 60, resulting in wait times of up to five hours as each polling place now served approximately 21,000 voters (Harris 2020).

Many scholars argue that there is significant evidence that moving or eliminating polling places increases costs of finding and getting to the polls and reduces participation (Brady and McNulty 2011; Yoder 2019). Stein and Vannahme have demonstrated that voter turnout, including engaging inconsistent voters, is strongly correlated to accessible and consistent polling locations (2008). Brady and McNulty demonstrated that habituation is a significant aide to voter turnout and that moving polling locations could reduce turnout by up to 2% (2011). Yoder found similar impacts in North Carolina (2017). Because many of the closed polling locations are in minority and economically disadvantaged communities, the impacts have both community and electoral consequences. Another tactic has been to close polling places in predominantly minority neighborhoods and consolidate them in majority white neighborhoods some distance away. Georgia has seen the use of such tactics over the past few years. The Georgia Chapter of the ACLU argues that the intent and effect is to suppress the African-American vote (Vasilogambros 2018). Changing polling locations to unfamiliar neighborhoods or environments is an effective tool of voter suppression (Vasilogambros 2018). While election officials and consultants claim that the consolidation, closure, and moving of polling places has not been done with racial or partisan motivation, the evidence would seem to support the idea that no matter the intent, the impact had racial and partisan outcomes (Vasilogambros 2018).

Polling places themselves can have an influence on turnout. The selection of specific locations for polling—schools, churches, public buildings, fire halls—can influence voter turnout and votes on particular issues. Holding elections in facilities that have overt religious, political, or social identities can impact voters' willingness and comfort to go to the polls. Research and a number of recent cases highlight the impacts that particular polling locations have on voter concerns (Berger et al. 2008; Rutchick 2010; Vasilogambros 2018).

The threats of long lines, voter identification challenges, limited voting information, changed polling places, and other impediments increase the perceived costs of participation. This is far more influential on participation for minorities and the economically disadvantaged as issues such as polling location, commuting, public transportation, atypical work schedules, and childcare are far more likely to hobble efforts to engage in voting. Early voting and mail-in voting are often promoted as possible solutions to these many election day and polling place barriers. The expansion of early voting and mail-in voting has also been notable over the past two decades. However, communities with large minority and economically disadvantaged populations are more dependent on polling places than mail-in ballots (Klain et al. 2020). Voter information tends to be lower in these communities and the procedures and deadlines to request mail-in ballots provide significant barriers. Even mail-in ballots are not safe from inequality. The ACLU of Florida has found that black and Latino voters were more than two times likely to have mail-in ballots rejected than white voters due to voter errors and state processing procedures (Harris 2020). In 2016, the United States Election Assistance Commission reported that more than 300,000 mail-in ballots were rejected (Harris 2020). There have been attempts to block or restrict certain voters from early voting even when allowed by law. In 2018, Florida election officials blocked early voting at locations near college and university campuses with a clear effort to limit mostly left-leaning voters from being able to cast early ballots (Vasilogambros 2018).

To this point, this chapter has mostly focused on well-documented and explored issues of voter registration and ballot access barriers for minority and economically disadvantaged citizens. Registration barriers such as criminal disenfranchisement, informational and procedural costs, purging of voter rolls, and rejection of registration applications clearly impact minority and low-income citizens more greatly than whites and higher income citizens. Once registered, gaining access to the ballot on election day and having that vote count are also at higher risk for minorities and low-income voters. Voter identification laws, closing and moving of polling locations, long lines and wait times, rejection of mail-in ballots, and other election day obstacles fall decisively more often on these groups. To some extent, despite rigorous debates among researchers and policymakers, the overwhelming evidence does paint a portrait of a system with serious and effective impediments to participation for many Americans. One variable that links all these practices, policies, laws, and phenomena is the overwhelming influence of state and local election officials and agencies. As this research argues, the decentralization of election law, voter registration, and election day operations to state and local governments is one of the central problems of American voting. The lack of conformity to the law, absence of uniformity, disproportionality in election resources, and variation in administration of voting procedures and policy is explained by the United States' unique level of decentralization of election and voting law and procedures. This decentralization is a deficit of the American electoral experience even in the best of times, and in times of natural disaster it can become far worse.

HYPER-DECENTRALIZATION

The decentralization of voter registration and ballot access is a critical feature of the American electoral system and one that explains the lack of uniformity and equality for many voters (Ewald 2009; Pettigrew 2017; Weinstein-Tull 2016). Ewald has labeled this system one of "hyper-federalization" (2009). The United States' constitution is the basis for decentralization of election law and supervision to state governments. The Elections Clause (Article I, Section 4) is the source of constitutional authority to regulate elections for Congress. The Clause empowers states to determine the "times, places, and manner" of congressional elections. These are not unlimited as the clause also grants Congress authority to "make or alter" rules (Morley and Tolson). The constitution ultimately grants expansive state prerogatives over registration and balloting elements of election law as well as delegation of election responsibilities to county, parish, town, or other municipal governments (Weinstein-Tull 2016; Ewald 2009). Ultimately this means that the United States has thousands of different election authorities with incredible variation in personnel, rules, laws, procedures, and resources (Kimball and Kropf 2006; Ewald 2009). There is not a single election and voting system in the United States, there are thousands.

Federal Power

Federal authority over elections and voting has mostly come from two sources, the constitutional (and its amendments) and federal laws. The Elections Clause and the 14th, 15th, 20th, and 26th amendments provide a significant basis of federal authority over election law and voting. Yet, the Election Clause does simultaneously empower the states with power over laws and management of the election and voting process. Beyond the constitution, most federal influence on elections is through federal election law.

Congress has exercised this power in numerous ways. It has established a single national Election Day for congressional elections and mandated that states with multiple representatives in the U.S. House divide themselves into congressional districts rather than all of their Representatives being at-large (Morley and Tolson). Many of the most powerful federal election laws have been passed in the last sixty years including the Voting Rights Act (VRA) of 1965, Uniformed and Overseas Citizen Absentee Voting Act (UOCAVA) of 1986, the National Voter Registration Act (NRVA) of 1993, the and the Help America Vote Act (HAVA) of 2002.

The most expansive federal legislation regarding election law and voting has been the VRA of 1965. Under Section 5 of the VRA, certain jurisdictions with a history of racial discrimination, mostly but not exclusively in the South, were required to submit all proposed voting changes to the United States Department of Justice in a process known as preclearance. Preclearance stemmed discriminatory voting changes prior to implementation by forcing states and local governments and election authorities to demonstrate that such laws would not have a discriminatory impact (Thurgood Marshall Institute 2016). This broad legislation meant that changes in polling places, ballot type, registration processes, voter identification requirements, and any other changes to registration and poll operations were subject to federal approval. In 2013, the United States Supreme Court nullified the preclearance process in the *Shelby County, Alabama v. Holder* decision. This opened the floodgates of electoral and voting changes at the state and local level that could be discriminatory (Thurgood Marshall Institute 2016). Many of the changes to polling places, photo identification laws, and other more restrictive policies and procedures have emerged in the post-Shelby environment (Thurgood Marshall Institute 2016). The expansion of such changes in enormous and growing.

The other major federal election legislations continue to regulate major aspects of voter registration, absentee ballots, voting machine technology, and accessibility for disabled persons. NRVA, also known as the Motor Voter Act, mandates states to offer voter registration opportunities at state agencies such as driver's license centers. UOCAVA requires states to transmit absentee ballots to overseas and military voters in a timely fashion to ensure their ballots count. HAVA, enacted after the 2000 election and the problems with hanging chads in Florida, required states to adopt voting machine technology and ensure accessibility. The weakening of the VRA by the court is critical, as it was the only federal legislation that targeted racial discrimination as the other acts are race-neutral (Weinstein-Tull 2016). While important to improving registration and ballot access, these acts do not explicitly work toward fixing the serious underlying issues of racial and class bias in the state and local election systems across the United States.

Other Supreme Court rulings and congressional actions have coincided with a major effort to erode existing centralization and federal power in favor of state and local authority. The *Raysor v. DeSantis* (2020) decision by the Supreme Court was a notable outcome that favored state authority. Following a 2018 referendum in Florida, resident citizens with prior felony convictions were to have franchise rights restored. Florida enacted a state law that prohibited such restoration of voting rights until they paid all court-imposed restitution, fees, and fines. The suit against the law alleged violations of the 1st, 14th, and 24th amendments to the U.S. Constitution, discrimination, and disenfranchisement on the basis of wealth, an illegal poll tax, and denied the right of due process (Brennan Center 2020). The new law clearly had significant impacts on minority and lower income residents. Further, Florida had no single system of reporting and clearing restitution, fees, and fines and hence would make the burden of clearance difficult for almost all former felons (Washington Post 2020). In *Gill v. Whitford (2018)*, the Supreme Court ruled that federal courts did not have the power to decide cases related to partisan gerrymandering, ending a Wisconsin lawsuit against the state using legislative maps drawn by Republicans in 2011 (Brennan Center 2018). While the courts would have authority over racial or ethnic gerrymandering, the decision illustrates the increasing willingness of the courts to side with state authority over important aspects of election law and process. In 2019, the House of Representatives passed new language for the VRA but it failed to gain traction in the Republican-held Senate and faced a possible veto by the President (Newkirk 2019).

State and Local Power

Both state and local officials play a great role in implementing state, federal, and local election laws and are responsible for the "nuts and bolts" of elections including registering voters, buying and maintaining voting equipment, printing ballots, hiring election workers, and choosing polling places (Kimball and Kropf 2006). While election law is dominantly set at the state level, the operations of voter registration and ballot access are delegated to county, parish, town, and municipal governments (Ewald 2005; Kimball and Kropf 2006). This allows application and enforcement of voter registration and ballot access laws to become highly dependent upon the knowledge, resources, training, and ethics of local election officials. As Ewald and others have argued, the lack of uniformity, knowledge, and application of state and federal laws on criminal disenfranchisement, voter registration, and ballot access is a fundamental problem (Ewald 2006, 2009; Weinstein-Tull 2016). The decentralization of voter registration and ballot access to states, counties, municipalities, and even specific polling locations creates an environment in which lack of training, lack of knowledge, and partisanship may effectively disenfranchise citizens with legitimate voting rights (Ewald 2005, 2009). While Ewald found the overwhelming majority of local officials interviewed were eager to understand the law, implement it fairly, and facilitate voting by everyone eligible under state law, it is also clear that not all such officials may hold such ethical standards or be free from partisan influence (Ewald 2005). That election rules and procedures may be manipulated for partisan and political gain has been a significant concern and with growing evidence (Kimball and Kropf 2006; Thurgood Marshall Institute 2016).

The selection of election officials and polling place works is considerably diverse and non-uniform even within states. Some local election officials are elected but most are appointed (Kimball and Kropf 2006; Fisher and Coleman 2008). Ewald's research illuminates that local election officials and registrars between and within states demonstrated a significant lack of knowledge, uniformity, and conformity to their state's voter eligibility laws (Ewald 2005, 2009). While Ewald's research was initially in regards to criminal disenfranchisement and its implications, the findings speak to the larger inconsistencies and ignorance of election officials at the municipal, county, and state levels in applying existing voter laws appropriately. Ewald's findings conclude that election officials at the county, town, or other municipal level are often ignorant of basic criminal/felony eligibility laws and interpret and enforce existing laws inconsistently (Ewald 2005, 2009). In his surveys, well over a third of the local election officials were unable to correctly describe the eligibility laws of their state. Among those that misidentified existing laws, over 85% did not know the eligibility standard or specified that the law was more restrictive than was actually the case (Ewald 2005). Given the wide lack of proper knowledge and application of voting laws in the area of criminal disenfranchisement not surprisingly the same officials are also misapplying or misinterpreting other voter eligibility, registration, and ballot access laws (Ewald 2005, 2009; Weinstein-Tull 2016).

Pettigrew argues that local election officials do a worse job serving minority precincts than white ones. Wait times at precincts within the same town or municipality reflect a serious "racial gap" (Pettigrew 2017). Pettigrew further argues that election officials provide more poll workers and voting machines to white precincts than minority ones (2017). Local governments are often constrained by the availability of poll workers, machines, and resources for elections. Yet, even in such communities the white voting precincts receive more resources than comparable minority districts (Pettigrew 2017). The level of racial discrimination and unequal treatment is a symptom of the fragmented and decentralized voting system of the states, counties, towns, and other municipalities used in the United States.

Citizens from lower socioeconomic status also are less likely to file complaints with the government and hence election officials can under-allocate resources to minority and poorer districts (Pettigrew 2017). Officials also respond to inquiries from Latino and Arab-Muslim Americans citizens at lower rates than with whites (Hughes et al. 2019; White et al. 2014). Hughes et al. demonstrate that bias against Latino and Arab-Muslim Americans by local election officials and bureaucrats (Hughes et al. 2019; White et al. 2014). Hughes et al. demonstrated that local election officials consciously or unconsciously demonstrated bias against minority group citizens (Hughes et al. 2019).

The overall pattern of election and voting management in the United States is one of "hyper-federalization" and fragmented intergovernmental responsibility and authority (Ewald 2009). Even prior to 2013, the "crazy quilt" of election and voting management and administration in the United States was fraught with inconsistency, non-conformity to law, and bias in many forms (Ewald 2006, 2009). The increasing decentralization of prerogatives to state and local governments with the voiding of parts of the VRA has intensified the shift from federal to state and local authority. The results of this sea change are the implementation of more registration and ballot obstacles that are far more likely to impact minorities and the economically disadvantaged (Thurgood Marshall Institute 2016). The enormous evidence and literature on issues of registration and ballot access must be viewed through the lens of American election and voting institutions. Without the heavily decentralized and fragmented election and voting system, such unequal variations would be far less likely and less influential. Under normal conditions, the current model of American elections and voting has exhibited even greater inequality and inaccessibility. Under emergency conditions, the combination of highly decentralized election and voting management with increasing barriers to registration and voting could imperil the functionality and credibility of American democracy.

THE IMPACT OF NATURAL DISASTERS
ON REGISTRATION AND VOTING

Previous sections of this chapter have argued that the hyper-decentralization of voter registration and ballot access to state and local governments are a primary source of racial, ethnic, and class bias. The increasing levels of disparity and lack of uniformity between and within states is a product of decreasing federal oversight and authority over registration and voting rules through congressional inaction and judicial rulings. With thousands of electoral districts in the United States with extraordinary variations in levels of professionalism, financial resources, training, equipment, personnel, laws, policies, and procedural norms, the American system of election and voting administration and management has enormous vulnerabilities and inequalities even in non-emergency times.

Natural disasters are extraordinary events that are becoming more ordinary. Natural disasters stress the resources of the local and state governments in numerous ways including policing, emergency services, sanitation, social and human services, education, housing, fire and medical services, and in every other imaginable function of government. Hurricanes, tornados, wildfires, earthquakes, flooding, and pandemics destroy and degrade not just communities but also the governments of those communities. It should not come as a surprise that voter and election services are substantially at risk during times of natural disaster. Destruction of facilities, loss of resources and equipment, loss and dislocation of essential personnel, loss of records, reassignment of resources to other agencies, and innumerable other consequences of natural disasters impede adequate functions of most local and state government agencies during times of disaster. Trying to sustain voter registration and polling operations in the midst or wake of a natural disaster is burdened by these substantial challenges.

Natural disasters and other emergencies do suppress voter participation due to inaccessible, closed, and relocated polling places. Additional limitations on voters and poll workers ability to get to polling places, and power outages also are significant impediments to elections. Voters who are irregular or infrequent voters are even less likely to participate under such conditions (Stein 2015). For most regular and frequent voters, the obstacles of voting during or immediately after natural disasters and emergencies are dependent upon the responses of state and local election officials. State and local election officials can mitigate the impact by allowing flexibility in ballot submission, extension of voting times and days (such as early voting), mail-in voting, expanding voting locations, and trying to minimize disruptions to the normal polling locations (Stein 2015). States and localities that allow early voting, allow voters to vote at numerous locations throughout the jurisdiction, and otherwise increase flexibility tend to sustain turnout even after natural disasters (Stein 2015). In the case of Hurricane Sandy, few of the ten impacted states initially allowed early or mail-in voting. The Hurricane made landfall on October 29, 2012 limiting the ability to request absentee ballots as the deadline had long passed and the election was to be held in just over a week on November 6. Stein identified that when local election officials were able to keep the locations, staffing, and number of polling places consistent, voter participation was stronger (2015).

The existing decentralized institutions of voter registration and ballot access are the primary culprits in increased limits to ballot access in normal times but can become even more effective barriers in the aftermaths of natural disasters. During and following natural disasters, voter registration and ballot access are hobbled in several ways and mirror the many issues discussed earlier. The voter registration process is problematized by dislocated citizens, personnel shortages in local and state election offices, destroyed equipment, lost files and paperwork, disruptions to mail service, and voter residency questions. Polling place operations are even more impacted. The movement and reduction of polling places, the loss of identification documents for voters, dislocation of voters within and outside the region, fewer available poll workers, longer lines and wait times, and other obstacles increase the informational and procedural costs for citizens. These conditions tend to afflict minority and economically disadvantaged voters to greater extents than white and more affluent ones.

Because of the highly decentralized system of election and voting administration and management in the United States, states and local governments demonstrate a remarkable inconsistency and nonuniformity in response to natural disasters. While most states have election laws and procedures in place for such circumstances, reviews of such laws and policies illuminate that local election authorities retain significant autonomy and prerogative (Stein 2015; NCSL 2020; Morely 2018). In the last twenty years, the empirical evidence of natural disasters, terrorism, and public health emergencies impacting registration and voting has grown dramatically. This reflects not only the potential increase in incidence of natural disasters and other emergencies but also the increasing legal, political, and policy interest in the impacts and responses to emergencies and elections. The increased interest and demand by policymakers to address threats of natural disasters and public health threats to voter registration and ballot access is notable. Morley argues that the U.S. electoral system is one that is highly vulnerable to threats from natural disasters, terrorism, and other calamities and that many states lack adequate laws and procedures to respond to such crises (Morley 2018). The intervention of the courts to settle election disputes in the wake of natural disasters is commonplace, highlighting the institutional weakness and incompleteness of such state and local laws and policies (Morley 2018).

Cataloging the instances of natural disasters and their impact on voter registration and ballot access cannot take place here yet the mounting and voluminous evidence from just the past two decades is remarkable. The following cases are notable and emblematic of the kinds of threats and responses that state and local election officials have and will continue to face. For instance, the terrorist attacks on September 11, 2001 disrupted primary election day for New York State and the New York mayoral primary was halted mid-vote. The New York state legislature met in special session a few days later and approved a rescheduling of all state primaries for September 25, 2001 (Nagourney 2001).

Numerous studies illustrated that areas of New Orleans that suffered the most severe flooding during Hurricane Katrina saw significant decreases in voter participation over several years. The relocation of victims to other parts of the city, state, and out of state created significant informational and procedural barriers for voting in subsequent elections (Sinclair et al. 2011). Displaced citizens are one of the largest issues for post-natural disaster registration and ballot access. After Hurricane Katrina, 400,000 registered voters from Louisiana relocated out of the state. While initial plans by the Secretary of State sought an expansive effort to make it easier for these citizens to vote in the postponed 2005 and 2006 elections, the state legislature scaled down such efforts supposedly based on costs and fraud concerns (Roy 2007). Ultimately, the state response created much higher informational and procedural costs for displaced voters living outside the state. Given the ethnic and class identifiers of this group—mostly African-American and economically disadvantaged, the effects of Louisiana's response to Katrina had significant political consequences for the 2005 and subsequent elections. The impact had a significant statewide impact on the overall balance between dominantly Democratic parishes in and around New Orleans and the dominantly Republican northern parishes (Roy 2007).

Hurricane Sandy made landfall less than 10 days before the elections in November 2012. The impact was felt in ten states along the Atlantic seaboard with varying levels of damage. The hurricane exemplified the differential responses between and within states to respond to the disaster. Hurricane Sandy prompted emergency voting measures in New York and New Jersey that were mostly effective and saw the vast majority of voters able to access the ballot (Kaplan 2013; Stein 2015). States and local municipalities that allowed early voting and sustained polling places with sufficient staffing saw relatively normal levels of turnout (Stein 2015). States and municipalities that restricted early voting, closed or relocated polling places, reduced personnel and increased wait times add to the already problematic obstacles and barriers to registration and voting. Stein discovered that local responses to Hurricane Sandy in 2012 varied, but those that allowed more flexibility and sustained existing polling places mitigated lower turnout (2015). In 2018, Hurricane Florence disrupted voter registration and early voting in North Carolina while Hurricane Michael had similar impacts in parts of Georgia and Florida (Slack 2018).

In the spring of 2020, governors and state election officials postponed and rescheduled primary elections across the United States due to the coronavirus pandemic. In Wisconsin, many poll workers would not work the primary due to fears from the coronavirus leading to more limited polling locations and long wait (Harris 2020). Voters in Milwaukee, the most ethnically diverse city in mostly white Wisconsin, had only five polling places compared to the typical 180 before the pandemic (Klain et al. 2020). Long lines in Arizona, Kentucky, Georgia, Wisconsin, and other states were products of significantly reduced polling places, fewer poll workers, and state and local decisions that massively increased costs of participation. As an interesting counter-example, Singapore held its national elections in the midst of the pandemic in July 2020. Rather than reduce polling locations and add restrictions, it allowed citizens to use passports instead of having to obtain new identity cards and added additional polling locations to allow for social distancing and to make the perceived costs and risks from voting lower (Lee 2020).

What we have learned from these and many other cases is that natural disasters may create conditions that are likely to impact voter registration and ballot access in many critical ways.

- Limiting the voter registration process by interrupting and shortening registration periods and making deadlines more difficult to meet
- Disrupting processing of voter registration applications due to personnel and resource shortages at state and county election offices
- Creating questions and issues of residency for displaced citizens, increasing the opportunities for mistakes and misapplication of existing law by local election officials
- Creating costs and uncertainties about eligibility to vote due to displacement
- Creating opportunities for improper purging of voter rolls due to displacement and misclassification of voters and residents
- Creating increased informational and procedural costs of registration process for citizens
- Decreasing personnel for polling places leading to consolidation, closure, and movement of polling places, increasing costs of voting
- Creating long lines and long wait times due to less personnel and fewer polling places
- Creating costs and uncertainties about eligibility to vote due to lost identification documents

The overall impacts of natural disasters on registration and ballot access are certainly magnifications of already existent problems in state and locally run election systems. Natural disasters also create opportunities for partisan state and local officials to game the system for particular electoral results. Effective disenfranchisement of minority and economically disadvantaged citizens was already a serious problem even without the impact of natural disasters. As we have seen in examples ranging from Hurricane Katrina to the coronavirus pandemic of 2020, state and local election officials may undertake changes to the registration and ballot access conditions that have extraordinary impacts on the ability of minorities and the economically disadvantaged to participate.

CONCLUSION

This research has sought to illuminate the existent and growing evidence and scholarship that links the titanic levels of decentralization in the American system of elections and voting administration to the increasing marginalization and exclusion of minority and economically disadvantaged voters in times of normalcy as well as in times of calamity. As other works in this volume have argued and demonstrated, categorical inequality is strongly correlated to far more sizeable and critical impacts from natural disasters than other groups of citizens. Many of the institutions created by American society and its political systems replicate and reinforce patterns of discrimination, bias, and inequality whether intended or not. These institutions, when stressed by the impact of natural disasters, public health threats, and other calamities tend to further magnify and reinforce such inequality.

The enormous fragmentation and decentralization of the American election and voting system is fraught with inconsistency, inequality, non-conformity to the law, and is ripe for both mismanagement and appropriation by partisan forces. Natural disasters create additional opportunities for both dysfunction and hijacking by partisan actors. Many recent cases of natural disasters and pandemics illustrate how partisan political elites and election officials can further disenfranchise minority and low-income voters. The impact between times of normalcy and emergency is one that is difficult to measure but it certainly present. Emergencies are political opportunities. With the growing incidence of natural disasters and the sizeable evidence from the 2020 pandemic responses available to researchers, the ability to measure the electoral and voting impact should become even more robust.

In terms of policy, the fair and equal implementation and application of voting laws by state and local officials is a critical problem of American democracy. As Ewald suggests, "haphazard administration of suffrage rules should be of concern to lawmakers and others interested in guaranteeing that our basic citizenship" rights are enforced (Ewald 2006). State and federal level policy could address and solve registration and ballot access restrictions in times of normalcy and natural disaster. The increasing impacts on elections by hurricanes and, in 2020, pandemic threats has moved federal, state, and local election officials and policymakers to put greater efforts into developing, implementing, and institutionalizing intergovernmental plans for voting during emergencies. Discussion and planning for how to protect electoral activities from such threats has become a more serious concern of the

Department of Homeland Security, the NCSL, the NASS, and policymakers at all levels of government.

While federal law has made efforts to address the inequalities and inconsistency of the localized voting system through the VRA, NVRA, HAVA, and other acts, these have fallen far short of creating a uniform and cohesive set of institutions to better manage American voter registration and ballot access. HAVA is illustrative of these challenges. HAVA implementation was far slower than expected and parts of the old systems continue to survive in many states despite eighteen years since its passage. Even under the "new" rules, local registrars continue to have the authority to purge individuals from the rolls in most states and most operational policies and procedures give local and state election officials broad latitude and discretion (Weinstein-Tull 2016).

The National Conference of State Legislatures (NCSL) has cataloged the existing election emergency laws across the fifty states. Forty-five states have some statutes to deal with election day emergencies, but there is "little consistency" between them and under what circumstances they come into effect and what actions could then be taken (NCSL 2020). The options most found in these disparate laws and policies include options for delaying and rescheduling elections, relocation of polling places, and combinations of the two. California, Florida, Oklahoma, and Virginia have the most expansive statutes (NCSL 2020). Within the differentiated state laws and plans is an extraordinarily inconsistent pattern of authorities given to governors, state election officials, and local election officers. In Arkansas, only county election boards may change the location of a polling place due to an emergency but there was no statewide authority to delay or reschedule an election. In California, the Secretary of State is empowered to enforce wide-ranging procedures and guidelines for voting, polling places can be moved but with restrictions mandating that the new location be as close as possible to the previous poll and that notices must be posted county-wide, satellite voting locations can be established, and other procedures. Wisconsin had no existing state-level statutes prior to 2020 (NCSL 2020).

The National Association of Secretaries of State (NASS) report, entitled States Laws & Practices for the Emergency Management of Elections provides guidance to the Secretaries of State, typically responsible for managing elections at the state level and overseeing state electoral and voting law. This was initially prompted by the impact of Hurricane Sandy in 2012 on the elections held in ten affected states less than ten days later. The report speaks mostly in generalities about he needs to communicate and coordinate with local and federal emergency management officials but also provides best practices for states attempting to plan or hold elections that have been affected by natural disasters (NASS 2017). However, it falls well short of any kind of binding, uniform, or consistent set of practices and expectations.

One common suggestion is to take election management out of the hands of partisan politicians by creating non-partisan committees and commissions in each state. While generally popular with voters, these commissions are actually not commonly used (Kimball and Kropf 2006). Such commissions would also not solve the remarkable variation between and within states that create many of the obstacles to equal treatment under existing election and voting laws.

In March 2020, in response to the ongoing coronavirus pandemic, Senators Klobuchar (Minnesota) and Wyden (Oregon) introduced the Natural Disaster and Emergency Ballot Act (NDEBA) of 2020. The bill was referred to committee where it has languished. The proposal created some important mandates on states in regards to elections and voting during and after natural disasters, pandemics, and other emergencies. Some of the key provisions include the following:

- Requirements that states create and maintain contingency plans for federal elections in the event of natural disasters and pandemics that include health and safety concerns of poll works and voters
- Absentee ballot requests must be available online
- Amending HAVA by mandating early voting in all future federal elections, expansion of vote by mail, online ballot requests, extend the counting of mailed ballots up to ten days past the election date
- Requiring postage paid envelopes for all voter registration and absentee ballot applications
- Development and establishment of a ballot tracking system by 2024 (with federal reimbursement)
- Additional funding for the Election Assistance Commission to provide resources to states to meet these new rules (S.3529: Natural Disaster and Emergency Ballot Act of 2020)

NDEBA would provide some key federal oversight of state and local registration and voting laws and procedures as well as providing some federal subsidy for such changes. But much like NVRA, HAVA, UOCAVA, and other acts, it still allows significant variation among the states that would still have nearly unlimited power to delegate such responsibilities to county and local election offices. Like most other acts, it does lack effective and mandatory mechanisms for reporting from the local to the state and then to the federal levels. Effective federal law to address inequalities at the state and local levels of election management, in times of normalcy and calamity, would need to promote and provide far more uniformity and regulatory power from the federal level. Given the current tendencies of the state governments, the federal courts, Congress, and the constitutional bases of state authority, a new law to mandate such uniformity built upon the basis of the VRA of 1965 seems very unlikely.

The goal of this research was to provide an institutional lens by which to understand how the substantial decentralization of the American election and voting systems leads to unequal outcomes for voters in both normal and emergency periods. To understand both the causes and solutions to the dilemmas of voter registration and ballot access in normal times and while under the threat of natural disaster, an intergovernmental approach and understanding is required. With increased threats and incidence of natural disaster and public health emergencies, the need to develop and implement substantive intergovernmental institutions, procedures, and resources to address equal access to voter registrations and the ballot are critical. Without understanding the constitutional, legal, and political complexity of the American election and voting system, efforts to address these critical threats will be impossible to craft.

REFERENCES

Avery, James M., and Mark Peffley. 2005. "Voter Registration Requirements, Voter Turnout, and Welfare Eligibility Policy: Class Bias Matters." *State Politics & Policy Quarterly* 5, 1 (March): 47–67. doi: 10.1177/153244000500500103.

Barreto, Matt A., Stephen Nuño, Gabriel R. Sanchez, and Hannah L. Walker. 2019. "The Racial Implications of Voter Identification Laws in America." *American Politics Research* 47, 2: 238–249.

Berger, Jonah, Marc Meredith, and S. Christian Wheeler. 2008. "Contextual Priming: Where People Vote Affects How They Vote." *Proceedings of the National Academy of Sciences* 105, 26 (July 1): 8846–8849.

Bhatt, Rachana, Evgenia Dechter, and Richard Holden. 2020. "Registration Costs and Voter Turnout." *Journal of Economic Behavior & Organization* 176: 91–104. doi: 10.1016/j.jebo.2020.04.017.

Brady, Henry E., and John E. McNulty. 2011. "Turning Out to Vote: The Costs of Finding and Getting to the Polling Place." *The American Political Science Review* 105, 1: 115–134. Accessed August 1, 2020. doi: 10.2307/41480830.

Brater, Jonathan. 2018. *Voter Purges: The Risks in 2018*. New York: The Brennan Center for Justice. February 27, 2018. https://www.brennancenter.org/sites/default/files/2019-08/Report_Voter_Purges_The_Risks_in_2018.pdf

The Brennan Center. 2019. "Gill v. Whitford." July 3, 2019. Accessed July 30, 2020. https://www.brennancenter.org/our-work/court-cases/gill-v-whitford

The Brennan Center. 2020. "Voting Rights Litigation 2020." July 28, 2020. Accessed July 30, 2020. https://www.brennancenter.org/our-work/court-cases/voting-rights-litigation-2020

Brown, Robert D., Robert A. Jackson, and Gerald C. Wright. 1999. "Registration, Turnout, and State Party Systems." *Political Research Quarterly* 52, 3 (September): 463–479. doi: 10.1177/106591299905200301.

Burden, Barry C. 2018. "Disagreement Over ID Requirements and Minority Voter Turnout." *The Journal of Politics* 80, 3: 1060–1063.

Cloward, Ricahrd A., and Frances Fox Piven. 1989. "Poverty and Electoral Power." *The Journal of Sociology and Social Welfare* 16, 4 (December): 99–105.

Erikson, Robert S., and Lorraine C. Minnite. 2009. "Modeling Problems in the Voter Identification—Voter Turnout Debate." *Election Law Journal: Rules, Politics, and Policy* 8, 2 (June): 85–101. Accessed April 29, 2009. doi: 10.1089/elj.2008.0017.

Ewald, Alec C. 2002. *The Ideological Paradox of Criminal Disenfranchisement Law in the United States*. Amherst: University of Massachusetts.

Ewald, Alec C. 2005. *A 'Crazy-Quilt' of Tiny Pieces: State and Local Administration of American Criminal Disenfranchisement Law*. Washington, DC. The Sentencing Project. November 2005.

Ewald, Alec C. 2009. *The Way We Vote: The Local Dimension of American Suffrage*. Nashville: Vanderbilt University Press.

Fisher, Eric A., and Kevin J. Coleman. 2008. *Election Reform and Local Election Officials: Results of Two National Surveys*. Washington, DC: Congressional Research Service. February 7, 2008.

Franko, William W., Nathan J. Kelly, and Christopher Witko. 2016. "Class Bias in Voter Turnout, Representation, and Income Inequality." *Perspectives on Politics* 14, 2 (June): 351–368.

Gidengil, Elisabeth, Hanna Wass, and Maria Valaste. 2016. "Political Socialization and Voting: The Parent–Child Link in Turnout." *Political Research Quarterly* 69, 2: 373–383. doi: 10.1177/1065912916640900.

Graham, David A. 2013. "Here's Why Black People Have to Wait Twice as Long to Vote as Whites." *The Atlantic*. April 8, 2013. Accessed July 20, 2020. https://www.theatlantic.com/politics/archive/2013/04/heres-why-black-people-have-to-wait-twice-as-long-to-vote-as-whites/274791/

Grimmer, Justin, Eitan Hersh, Marc Meredith, Jonathan Mummolo, and Clayton Nall. 2018. "Obstacles to Estimating Voter ID Laws' Effect on Turnout." *The Journal of Politics* 80, 3: 1045–1051.

Hajnal, Zoltan, John Kuk, and Nazita Lajevardi. 2018. "We All Agree: Strict Voter ID Laws Disproportionately Burden Minorities." *The Journal of Politics* 80, 3: 1052–1059.

Hajnal, Zoltan, Nazita Lajevardi, and Lindsay Nielson. 2017. "Voter Identification Laws and the Suppression of Minority Votes." *The Journal of Politics* 79, 2: 363–379.

Hanrahan, Patricia. 1994. "No Home? No Vote." *Human Rights: Journal of the Section of Individual Rights & Responsibilities* 21: 8–30.

Harris, Adam. 2020. "The Voting Disaster Ahead." *The Atlantic*. June 30, 2020. Accessed July 20, 2020. https://www.theatlantic.com/politics/archive/2020/06/voter-suppression-novembers-looming-election-crisis/613408/

Highton, Benjamin. 2017. "Voter Identification Laws and Turnout in the United States." *Annual Review of Political Science* 20 (May): 149–167. doi: 10.1146/annurev-polisci-051215-022822.

Hood, M. V., and Charles S. Bullock. 2012. "Much Ado About Nothing? An Empirical Assessment of the Georgia Voter Identification Statute." *State Politics & Policy Quarterly* 12, 4 (December): 394–414. doi: 10.1177/1532440012452279.

Hood, M. V., and Scott E. Buchanan. 2020. "Palmetto Postmortem: Examining the Effects of the South Carolina Voter Identification Statute." *Political Research Quarterly* 73, 2: 492–505.

Hughes, D. Alex, Micah Gell-Redman, Charles Crabtree, Natarajan Krishnaswami, Diana Rodenberger, and Guillermo Monge. 2019. "Persistent Bias Among Local Election Officials." *Journal of Experimental Political Science.* Cambridge University Press, 1–9. doi: 10.1017/XPS.2019.23.

Jackson, Robert A., Robert D. Brown, and Gerald C. Wright. 1998. "Registration, Turnout, and the Electoral Representativeness of U.S. State Electorates." *American Politics Quarterly* 26, 3 (July): 259–287. doi: 10.1177/1532673X9802600301.

Kaplan, Thomas. 2013. "Using Hurricane Sandy as a Lesson for Future Elections." *The New York Times.* November 13, 2013. www.nytimes.com%2F2013%2F11%2F13%2Fnyregion%2Flessons-from-hurricane-sandy-being-applied-to-election-planning.html&usg=AOvVaw0K_LkeCWBBVRuVtIVteo1-

Kimball, David C., and Martha Kropf. 2006. "The Street-Level Bureaucrats of Elections: Selection Methods for Local Election Officials." *Review of Policy Research* 23, 6 (November 21). doi: 10.1111/j.1541-1338.2006.00258.x.

Klain, Hannah, Kevin Morris, Max Feldman, and Rebecca Ayala. 2020. *Waiting to Vote: Racial Disparities in Election Day Experiences.* New York City: Brennan Center for Justice. June 3, 2020. Accessed July 15, 2020. https://www.brennancenter.org/sites/default/files/2020-06/6_02_WaitingtoVote_FINAL.pdf

Kuk, John, Zoltan Hajnal, and Nazita Lajevardi. 2020. "A Disproportionate Burden: Strict Voter Identification Laws and Minority Turnout." *Politics, Groups, and Identities* 66: 1–9.

Lee, Yen Nee. 2020. "5 Reasons Why Singapore's Upcoming General Election Is Worth Watching." *CNBC.com.* July 1, 2020. Accessed July 30, 2020. https://www.cnbc.com/2020/07/01/5-reasons-why-singapores-upcoming-general-election-is-worth-watching.html

Leighley, Jan E., and Jonathan Nagler. 1992. "Socioeconomic Class Bias in Turnout, 1964–1988: The Voters Remain the Same." *The American Political Science Review* 86, 3: 725–736. Accessed August 14, 2020. doi: 10.2307/1964134.

McDonald, Jared, and Michael Hanmer. 2019. "Understanding and Confronting Barriers to Youth Voting in America." *APSA Preprints.* doi: 10.33774/apsa-2019-42qw1.

Merivaki, Thessalia. 2019. "Access Denied? Investigating Voter Registration Rejections in Florida." *State Politics & Policy Quarterly* 19, 1 (March): 53–82. doi: 10.1177/1532440018800334.

Merivaki, Thessalia. 2020a. "Our Voter Rolls Are Cleaner Than Yours: Balancing Access and Integrity in Voter List Maintenance." *American Politics Research* 48, 5: 560–570.

Merivaki, Thessalia. 2020b. "Who Is Left Out? The Process of Validating Voter Registration Applications." *American Politics Research* (July). doi: 10.1177/1532673X20914613.

Merivaki, Thessalia, and Daniel A. Smith. 2020a. "Challenges in Voter Registration." In *The Future of Election Administration*, edited by Brown, Mitchell, Kathleen Hale, and Bridgett A. King. New York: Palgrave Macmillan. doi: 10.1007/978-3-030-14947-5.

Merivaki, Thessalia, and Daniel A. Smith. 2020b. "A Failsafe for Voters? Cast and Rejected Provisional Ballots in North Carolina." *Political Research Quarterly* 73, 1 (March): 65–78. doi: 10.1177/1065912919875816.

Morley, Michael T. 2018. "Election Emergencies: Voting in The Wake Of Natural Disasters and Terrorist Attacks." *Emory Law Journal* 67, 3: 545–617.

Morley, Michael T., and Franita Tolson. 2020. "Elections Clause." https://constitution center.org/interactive-constitution/interpretation/article-i/clauses/750

Nagler, Jonathan. 1991. "The Effect of Registration Laws and Education on U.S. Voter Turnout." *American Political Science Review* 85: 1393–1405.

Nagourney, Adam, 2011. "After the Attacks: The Election." *The New York Times*. September 14, 2001. www.nytimes.com%2F2001%2F09%2F14%2Fus%2Fafter -attacks-election-primary-rescheduled-for-sept-25-with-runoff-if-necessary.html& usg=AOvVaw3PFrWi-Hyr_VWpL29JGDiX

National Association of Secretaries of State. 2017. *State Laws and Practices for the Emergency Management of Elections*. Washington, DC: NASS. April 2017. Accessed June 30, 2020. http://www.nass.org/sites/default/files/surveys/2019-07/ report-NASS-emergency-preparedness-elections-apr2017.pdf

National Conference of State Legislatures. 2020. "Election Emergencies." April 7, 2020. Accessed July 10, 2020. https://www.ncsl.org/research/elections-and-campaigns/ election-emergencies.aspx

Newkirk II, Vann R. 2019. "The Democrats' New Voting-Rights Moment." *The Atlantic*. March 2, 2019. https://www.theatlantic.com/politics/archive/2019/03/ democrats-hope-restore-key-section-voting-rights-act/583969/

Nickerson, David W. 2015. "Do Voter Registration Drives Increase Participation? For Who and When?" *Journal of Politics* 77, 1: 88–101.

Pettigrew, Stephen. 2017. "The Racial Gap in Wait Times: Why Minority Precincts are Underserved by Local Election Officials." *Political Science Quarterly* 132, 3: 527–547.

Piven, Frances Fox, and Richard A. Cloward. 2000. *Why Americans Still Don't Vote: And Why Politicians Want It That Way*. Boston: Beacon Press.

Plutzer, Eric. 2002. "Becoming a Habitual Voter: Inertia, Resources, and Growth in Young Adulthood." *American Political Science Review* 96, 1: 41–56.

Roy, Maya. 2007. "The State of Democracy After Disaster: How to Maintain the Right to Vote for Displaced Citizens." *Southern California Interdisciplinary Law Journal* 17, 1: 203–230.

Rugeley, Cynthia, and Robert A. Jackson. 2009. "Getting on the Rolls: Analyzing the Effects of Lowered Barriers on Voter Registration." *State Politics & Policy Quarterly* 9, 1 (March): 56–78. doi: 10.1177/153244000900900103.

Rutchick, Abraham M. 2010. "Deus Ex Machina: The Influence of Polling Place on Voting Behavior." *Political Psychology* 31, 2 (April): 209–225. doi: 10.1111/j.1467-9221.2009.00749.x.

Ruth, Terrance, Jonathan Matusitz, and Demi Simi. 2017. "Ethics of Disenfranchisement and Voting Rights in the U.S.: Convicted Felons, the Homeless, and Immigrants." *American Journal of Criminal Justice* 56–68. doi: 10.1007/s12103-016-9346-6.

The Sentencing Project. 2010. *Losing the Vote: The Impact of Felony Disenfranchisement Laws in the United States*. New York: Human Rights Watch.

Sinclair, Betsy, Thad E. Hall, and R. Michael Alvarez. 2011. "Flooding the Vote: Hurricane Katrina and Voter Participation in New Orleans." *American Politics Research* 39, 5 (September): 921–957. doi: 10.1177/1532673X10386709.

Slack, Donovan. 2018. "Midterms: Hurricanes Leave Election Officials Scrambling as Tight Races Hang in the Balance." *USA Today*. October 19, 2018. https://www.usatoday.com/story/news/politics/2018/10/19/hurricanes-michael-and-florence-they-also-cause-midterm-damage/1676994002/

Stein, Robert M. 2015. "Election Administration During Natural Disasters and Emergencies: Hurricane Sandy and the 2012 Elections." *Election Law Journal* 14, 1: 66–73.

Stein, Robert M., and Greg Vonnahme. 2008. "Engaging the Unengaged Voter: Voter Centers and Voter Turnout." *Journal of Politics* 70: 1–11.

Thurgood Marshall Institute. 2016. *Democracy Diminished: State and Local Threats to Voting Post-Shelby County, Alabama v. Holder*. Washington, DC. NAACP Legal Defense Fund. https://tminstituteldf.org/wp-content/uploads/2017/08/Democracy -Diminished-State-and-Local-Voting-Changes-Post-Shelby-v.-Holder_4.pdf

The United States Congress. 2020. "S.3529 – Natural Disaster and Emergency Ballot Act of 2020." https://www.congress.gov/bill/116th-congress/senate-bill/3529?q=%7B%22search%22%3A%5B%22the+Natural+Disaster+and+Emergency+Ballot+Act+of+2020%22%5D%7D&s=1&r=1

Vasilogambros, Matt. 2018. "Polling Places Remain a Target Ahead of November Elections." *Pew Stateline*. September 4, 2018. https://www.pewtrusts.org/en/research-and-analysis/blogs/stateline/2018/09/04/polling-places-remain-a-target-ahead-of -november-elections

Verba, Sidney, Kay Lehman Schlozman, Henry Brady, and Norman H. Nie. 1993. "Citizen Activity: Who Participates? What Do They Say?" *American Political Science Review* 87, 2: 303–318. Cambridge University Press. doi: 10.2307/2939042.

Verba, Sydney, Kay Lehman Schlozman, and Nancy Burns. 2005. "Family Ties: Understanding the Intergenerational Transmission of Political Participation." In *The Social Logic of Politics: Personal Networks as Contexts for Political Behavior*, edited by Zuckerman, Alan, 95–114. Philadelphia: Temple University Press.

The Washington Post. 2020. "A Judge Says the GOP Can't Keep Florida Felons from Voting. But Lawmakers Will Keep Trying." May 28, 2020. https://www.washingtonpost.com/opinions/a-judge-says-the-gop-cant-keep-florida-felons-from-voting-but-lawmakers-will-keep-trying/2020/05/28/dc653f6e-a056-11ea-9590-1858a893bd59_story.html

Wattenberg, Martin P. 2002. *Where Have All The Voters Gone?* Cambridge: Harvard University Press.

Weil, Matthew, Charles Stewart III, Tim Harper, and Christopher Thomas. 2019. *The 2018 Voting Experience: Polling Place Lines.* Washington, DC. Bipartisan Policy Center. https://bipartisanpolicy.org/report/the-2018-voting-experience

Weinstein-Tull, Justin. 2016. "Election Law Federalism." *Michigan Law Review* 114, 5 (March): 747–802.

White, Ariel R., Noah L. Nathan, and Julie K. Faller. 2015. "What Do I Need to Vote? Bureaucratic Discretion and Discrimination by Local Election Officials." *American Political Science Review* 109, 1: 129–142. Cambridge University Press. doi: 10.1017/S0003055414000562.

Wolfinger, Raymond E., and Jonathan Hoffman. 2001. "Registering and Voting with Motor Voter." *PS: Political Science and Politics* 34, 1 (March): 85–92.

Xu, Jun. 2005. "Why Do Minorities Participate Less? The Effects of Immigration, Education, and Electoral Process on Asian American Voter Registration and Turnout." *Social Science Research* 34, 4: 682–702. doi: 10.1016/j.ssresearch.2004.11.002.

Yoder, Jesse. 2018. "How Polling Place Changes Reduce Turnout: Evidence from Administrative Data in North Carolina." *SSRN Electronic Journal.* May 30, 2018. http://dx.doi.org/10.2139/ssrn.3178184

Chapter 4

Judging Worthiness

Hurricane María, Puerto Ricans, and the Articulation of American National Identity

Amílcar Antonio Barreto

We expect natural disasters to present us the opportunity to examine the efficiency with which governments rescue the injured, provide for the immediate material needs of the displaced, and how they engage in crucial post-catastrophe restoration projects. Less apparent is how these events help us scrutinize competing notions of citizenship. According to the popular narrative, national identity in the United States is based upon a shared commitment to democratic principles, not ascriptive characteristics. Others counter that this outlook is exceedingly naïve. Let us examine the federal government's response to the devastation in Puerto Rico wrought by Hurricane María in 2017. U.S. president Donald Trump's reaction to the crisis spoke volumes about the continued racialization of some citizens and the selectiveness of national authenticity and belonging.

Rather than focusing on quickly allaying the suffering of several million U.S. citizens—as was the case with hurricanes on the U.S. mainland—the White House repeatedly chastised Puerto Rico's government for its economic mismanagement. It pushed the message that Hurricane María was not *that bad*. The administration downplayed the damage and minimized fatalities, and insisted that only sixteen died (Landler 2017). While a study published in the *New England Journal of Medicine* estimated a death toll of over four thousand (Kishore et al. 2018). Those who dared challenge Trump's narrative, particularly San Juan's Mayor Carmen Yulín Cruz, were abruptly, viciously and personally attacked. The federal government's flaccid mobilization of resources, especially in the early days of the crisis, underscored that policymakers' responses to catastrophes are uneven. Beyond material harm and basic human needs, political operatives take into account citizens' relative *worthiness*. Donald Trump's responses to the Hurricane María crisis speaks to a well-entrenched process that racializes Puerto Ricans, as well as other people of color in the United States who are branded a lower order of citizen who should be grateful for what they receive.

A NATURAL DISASTER AND
PRESIDENTIAL (IN)ACTION

Leaving meteorology to a side for one moment, Puerto Rico's economic crisis already portended a gloomy forecast. As Calhoun (2010, 30) observed, the term "emergency" focuses attention on the event at hand rather than the conditions that created it. In the 1990s Congress retracted the federal tax incentives that supplied the lifeblood of Puerto Rico's industrial economy—a budgetary model based on *Factories and Foodstamps* (Weisskoff 1985). Congress did so because "Puerto Rico's strategic function in advancing American geopolitical and ideological goals in its confrontation with the Soviet Union became anachronistic and inconsequential as the Cold War dissolved" (Cabán 2018, 4). As manufacturing plants closed tens of thousands of unemployed Puerto Ricans packed their bags and relocated to the U.S. mainland, further eroding the government's tax base (Feliciano 2018). To be clear, federal policymakers were not solely responsible for this fiasco. Obsessed with the next election, one Commonwealth administration after another spent far more than was prudent. This reckless practice left islanders with an unpayable debt of $72 billion ("How to Save" 2016). In light of economic conditions Puerto Rico's government was unable to make expensive, albeit desperately needed, upgrades to the island's infrastructure—particularly its electrical grid (Sullivan 2018).

In June 2015, Governor Alejandro García-Padilla announced that the territorial government was incapable of paying its debts. Bush's *compassionate conservative* rhetoric had long since evaporated, and in its stead Washington found inspiration in philosopher Michel Foucault (1995): *Discipline and Punishment*. Congress passed the 2016 Puerto Rico Oversight, Management, and Economic Stability Act (PROMESA)—a law that superimposed an appointed Fiscal Oversight and Management Board above the Commonwealth's elected government in all fiscal matters.[1] Since then Puerto Rico has been on a fiscal leash. This federal statute ended any lingering doubt over the supposed autonomy invested in the 1952 Commonwealth constitution (Meléndez 2018, 67).

To the island's fiscal and political woes, we add two natural catastrophes in September 2017. Hurricane Irma grazed the island early that month. A couple of weeks later Hurricane María made a direct hit. Streets everywhere were clogged with trees and electrical poles. Rural communities were effectively isolated. While the first cyclone knocked out power to seventy percent of Puerto Rican households its successor—a category five storm—smashed the power grid in its entirety (Ferré-Sadurní and Hartocollis 2017). Without electricity food in homes, restaurants and warehouses spoiled. Without current, many were forced to scramble for water as pumping stations stopped working. Medicines requiring refrigeration, such as insulin, had to be thrown away. And those in need of life-saving equipment were forced to do without.

The damage wrought by Hurricane María reminded many of Hurricane Katrina in 2005. As Nix-Stevenson (2013, 145) noted, there is nothing *natural* about disasters: "Nature provides the hazards—earthquakes, volcanic eruptions, floods and so on—but humans help create the disaster or crisis. We cannot prevent a tsunami, hurricane, or earthquake but we can prevent it from becoming a disaster or crisis." With self-imposed blinders, policymakers are inclined to ignore the early signs foretelling future emergencies (Calhoun 2010, 32). Federal officials were well aware of New Orleans's vulnerability to hurricanes. A year before Katrina made landfall FEMA (2004) anticipated much of the damage that would befall the *Big Easy* and the resources necessary to mitigate the cataclysm. By ignoring these warnings the Bush administration was complicit in laying the groundwork for an "unnatural disaster" (Marable 2008, ix). In hindsight, former president Bush (2010, 331) admitted that he erred by not deploying the 82nd Airborne immediately. Twelve years after Katrina the same self-imposed tunnel vision would have dire consequences on more than three million inhabitants of Puerto Rico.

The Trump administration's initial response to Hurricane María was lethargic and its attitude about the whole matter was *blasé*. Days passed before the federal government finally took this as a serious matter ("Puerto Rico Deserves" 2017). It was none other than Hillary Clinton who prodded the federal government to dispatch a military hospital ship to the island and send other vital aid with all due haste ("Hillary Clinton" 2017). Well versed in the island's political status Hilary Clinton had served as a Senator from New York—the state with the largest Puerto Rican community on the U.S. mainland (Barreto 2002, 54). Both Secretary Clinton ("Hillary Clinton" 2017) and the *New York Times* felt it necessary to remind the American public that Puerto Ricans were U.S. citizens ("Puerto Rico Is" 2017). Sadly, as one poll revealed, only slightly more than half of all Americans were aware of that fact (*Morning Call* 2017). On the one hand, ignorance of Puerto Ricans' status empowered the Trump administration to behave as if U.S. citizens were not impacted. On the other hand, even those Trump supporters who know Puerto Ricans are U.S. citizens are in no rush to come to the rescue of a people they don't consider to be *real* Americans. As Negrón-Muntaner (2019, 118) observed, "citizenship has never offered full protection for racialized, colonial, and otherwise minoritized legal citizens in the United States." Contrasting Trump and Clinton's responses to the same tragic event lends credence to the conjecture that the country's two major political parties are gravitating toward fundamentally different conceptualizations of American national identity—one civic, the other ethnoracial (Barreto and Napolio 2018).

As a gesture of good will, Trump finally announced that he would visit the island. Nevertheless, that pronouncement came with a now familiar reaction: shift blame onto others. Here the fault lay with Puerto Ricans themselves. After all, the island was, in Trump's words, "already suffering from broken infrastructure & massive debt" (Robles et al. 2017). His narrative omitted any mention of the federal government's contribution to the island's fiscal crisis while he unfeelingly brushed off human suffering. After all, in the Trumpian universe compassion—an extremely rare commodity—is reserved for *real* Americans. "We" truly suffer. Others *may* suffer, but not to the same degree. And it goes without saying, "we" are never responsible for anything wrong or anyone else's ineptitude.

Puerto Rico was not alone that year. Texas was recovering from Hurricane Harvey and Florida was picking up the pieces after Hurricane Irma. Yet, it was becoming apparent that the Trump administration viewed hurricane-inflicted damage differently depending on which U.S. jurisdiction was impacted ("Jorge Ramos" 2017; Vinik 2018). While Texas and Florida do harbor large Latino communities, they are not a part of his *base*. The benefits Texas and Florida Latinos received from these disaster was a fortuitous side effect of living in close proximity to the president's true constituents in two electorally critical states.

Puerto Rican politicians' responses were quite revealing. The new governor, Ricardo Rosselló, meekly ask for additional federal assistance. An ardent advocate of making Puerto Rico the fifty-first state, Rosselló was reluctant to risk losing Trump's support for his cherished cause. A year later Trump would come out openly against Puerto Rican statehood ("Donald Trump rechaza" 2018). In contrast, Carmen Yulín Cruz, the pro-commonwealth mayor of San Juan, was anything but shy (Rivera Cedeño 2017). Mayor Cruz reproached the White House exclaiming: "dammit, this is not a good news story. This is a 'people are dying' story" (Victor 2017). Once more, the White House pushed aside human anguish and scolded those who dared question Uncle Sam's beneficence. Unable to "get their workers to help" and wanting "everything to be done for them" the president simply accused Puerto Rico's politicians, particularly Mayor Cruz, of "poor leadership" (Delgado 2017). Reproaching Puerto Ricans who dared challenge his response to this hurricane was the soft version of a more virulent attack pattern. If not criminal, the *others* and their leaders are at least incompetent and languid. Accusations of laziness is a well-worn tactic used to write off the struggles of people of color (DeGenoa and Ramos-Zayas 2003, 36; Grosfoguel 2003, 10; Lundskow 2012, 533).

To justify his approach to the Hurricane María disaster Trump had to convince his followers that damage reports were overblown. He also felt the need to shift the blame on Puerto Ricans themselves. Strategically the White House tour bypassed hard-hit areas—the overwhelming majority of island— and focus instead on Guaynabo (Colón Dávila 2017). A suburb of San Juan, Guaynabo is Puerto Rico's wealthiest town. With wealth comes a robust infrastructure. Consequently, this city appeared to have suffered less devastation than the rest of the island. Lacking any empathy Trump again pointed the finger of blame: "Now I hate to tell you, Puerto Rico, but you've thrown our budget a little out of whack. We've spent a lot of money on Puerto Rico and that's fine, we've saved a lot of lives" (Costa 2017). One can summarize the tone of Trump's trip in the following manner: stop whining, go mop up the mess yourself, and get your finances in order.

Out of the entire Trump tour, one image stood out above all others. As if they were footballs, he tossed rolls of paper towels into a crowd of aid recipients. His gesture trivialized basic need items, treating them as little more than trinkets at a county fair (Pachecho Álvarez 2017). A week and a half later Trump announced that he was losing his patience, shifted more of the blame on Puerto Ricans, and warned that the federal government relief efforts would not remain indefinitely (Baker and Dickerson 2017). Mayor Cruz responded: "While you are amusing yourself throwing paper towels at us, your compatriots and the world are sending love and help our way. Condemn us to a slow death of nondrinkable water, lack of food, lack of medicine while you keep others eager to help from reaching us" (ibid).

The new game in town was a morose form of comparative suffering. Never one to forego the opportunity to show poor taste Trump started comparing the damage in Puerto Rico with "a real catastrophe like Katrina" where "hundreds and hundreds of people" died (Costa 2017). *Real* disasters happen at home. As the U.S. Supreme Court stated over a century ago, Puerto Rico was "a territory appurtenant and belonging to the United States, but not a part of the United States."[2] Trump's comparative disaster logic simply reinforced that idea. Repeatedly he insisted that Puerto Rico's death toll amounted to only sixteen victims (Landler 2017). Most of the Hurricane Katrina victims died as a direct result of the flooding. On the other hand, most Hurricane María victims in Puerto Rico passed away after the storm due to untreated illnesses and the inability to obtain adequate health care. It is estimated that the number of Hurricane María fatalities in Puerto Rico surpassed 4,000 (Kishore et al. 2018). While the federal government's response to the crisis was far from robust, many from the U.S. mainland tried their best to fill the void, including celebrity chef José Andrés.

Never mind that the official death count was obviously wrong, or that there were credible reports of the morgues being full across the island. What kind of person is proud of sixteen people dying? Only someone who could draw a line between "all your people" and "all of our people." Someone who didn't see Puerto Ricans as "our people" or real people at all, even though he was the president of all American citizens, including those in the Caribbean. (Andrés 2018, 109)

We recall Trump's categorization of Mexican immigrants on the campaign trails, and by extension Mexican Americans: "They're bringing drugs. They're bringing crime. They're rapists. And some, I assume, are good people" ("Here's Donald" 2015). For Trump and his followers, Puerto Ricans, like other Latinos and other people of color, are a lower order of Americans. As Molina-Guzmán (2019, 342) aptly noted, "Trump's rhetoric of toxic masculinity, a white masculine discourse in which women and ethnic and racial minorities are inherently inferior and expected to be subservient, further highlights the inherent power and authority of white patriarchal colonial logics." Maskovsky (2017, 434) labeled this phenomenon *white nationalist postracialism*—a tenet based on "reclaim[ing] the nation for white Americans while also denying an ideological investment in white supremacy." Latinos still get government assistance during calamities, but it's a second-class, hand-me-down version of the aid rendered to the truly *worthy*.

THE DESERVING: NARRATING
DISASTERS IN U.S. HISTORY

Studies of responses to natural disasters should prod us in the direction of comparison rather than exceptionalism. While federal appropriations for disaster relief date as far back as the late eighteenth century, congressional debates over Texas drought relief in the 1880s marked a major milestone in how the U.S. government would respond to future events (Dauber 2005, 394, 400). Assistance proponents employed a "disaster narrative" that framed the suffering as "needy through no fault of their own" (ibid. 400). Half a century later New Deal proponents would employ the same tactic, describing the economic tumult of the 1930s as an economic "disaster" (ibid., 442). Thus, they fashioned a spectacular event—a dreadful earthquake that lasted days, a monstrous hurricane that endured weeks. They invented the "Great Depression" (Landis 1999, 285).

In and of itself, framing events as disasters is inadequate. The suffering must be cast as protagonists playing the role of the *deserving*. As Essary and Ferney (2013, 97) contend: "Without theatrics, there would be no politics." Inherently, such a designation is ineffective without its thespian foil, the *undeserving*—a well-entrenched feature of the American welfare state (Gordon 2001, 15; Landis 1999, 261). For instance, following the Civil War Freedmen's Bureau advocates tried to bolster their cause by terming recently-freed slaves as "orphan children" and as a hard-working people who were "sober and industrious" (Dauber 2005, 415). Likewise, the debates over Social Security emphasized that its recipients were worthy because they "earned" their benefits (Gordon 2001, 16). Such a framework counters Calhoun (2010, 34) who contended that the "emergency imaginary" is thoroughly modern—one which is "disembedded from kinship, religion, nationality, and other webs of identity." For Gordon (2001, 14) human communities are "moral communities" that predicate assistance based on reputation and deservingness.

Just who are the deserving? Historically worthiness has been gendered, racialized (Gordon 2001, 16–20), and even commodified (Chasin 2000, 2).[3] At its inception, federal financial assistance programs such as Social Security were viewed primarily as a benefit for whites (Katznelson 2005). However, public support declined as they were increasingly associated with people of color who were stigmatized as the source of most out of wed childbirths (Gordon 2001, 19–22; Levin 2019, 47). As a general rule, the racist right eschews the blatant bigotry more common in previous eras in favor of a superficially softer variant, which jabs its victims via suggestion and innuendo—*dog whistle politics* (Haney-Lopez 2014). Attacking welfare become a convenient means to publicly attack people of color all the while denying any racial motivation (Gilens 1996). Similarly, Trump's attacks on Puerto Rican fiscal irresponsibility in the wake of Hurricane María all the while ignoring the severity of the devastation was a convenient way to racially frame the scenario (Morales 2019, 81–82) all the while denying its racist intent.

Analyses of media coverage of Hurricane Katrina aftermath echo these arguments. Many media outlets described New Orleans disaster victims with the same language used to depict looters (Tierney et al. 2006, 74). Those who plunder are inherently unworthy subjects, even if they are undergoing a catastrophe. The same brush strokes were used to paint all city residents. "Their government had forsaken them: they weren't citizens but castoffs, evacuees turned effortlessly, in language and life, into refugees" (Dyson 2005, 71–72). This term helped to paint a portrait of an unworthy community.

Charity begins at home, so the saying goes. And refugees are innately outsiders—they flee one home in pursuit of another. Banned from first-class citizenship, they get leftover generosity. Effectively, before anyone can be a refugee one must first be denaturalized (Sterett 2012, 233). Labeling a subset of citizens refugees is one way to rhetorically cut them off from their U.S. citizenship. Disturbingly, Ben-Porath and Shaker's (2010) study of responses to media stories of Hurricane Katrina victims suggests that whites were less likely to hold the federal government responsible for the high death count after seeing pictures of the deceased as opposed to those who did not see such images. The imagery of floating bodies in New Orleans helped to shatter the mythology of equality for all and the "fiction of living in a colorblind society" (Giroux 2007, 307).

Our discussion would be incomplete without taking into account the epitome of the undeserving—those who pose a threat. Foucault (1980, 1) commented: "those who are in power today want to use against us—in order to bring us back under control—the dual pressure of enemies invading from abroad and those who threaten us at home." Recurringly people of color have been thrust into that dubious role: "race has been the ever present shadow in Western political thought and practice, especially when it comes to imagining the inhumanity of, or rule over, foreign peoples" (Mbembe 2003, 17). And no community is alienated more than African Americans—the quintessential *anticitizens* (Olson 2004, 43). Menacing images of a murderous O. J. Simpson or an "out of control" Rodney King reinforce such stereotypes (Fiske 1996, 142; Gabriel 1998, 130). As innately unworthy subjects, the deaths of those who pose a racial threat to society is analogized to the removal of cancerous growth. As Foucault (2003, 258) put it, "racism justifies the death-function in the economy of biopower by appealing to the principle that the death of others makes one biologically stronger."

RACIALIZING GEOGRAPHY

Emergency relief efforts are hardly value neutral. That's because, as Kroll-Smith and Brown-Jeffy (2013, 534) stated, catastrophic events "do not occur in historical vacuums; rather they take shape and form in part through the social, political, and economic forces in play at the moment of impact." And those forces are, cartographically, very uneven. Historically white-occupied spaces have been construed as civilized whereas their non-white equivalents have been depicted as settings in a Hobbesian state of nature (Goldberg 2002, 39–47). Colonial powers embraced the philosophy that the overseas natives were incapable of governing themselves and in need of the civilizing graces of European rule (Calhoun 2010, 39–40). "Space was therefore the raw material of sovereignty and the violence it carried with it. Sovereignty meant occupation, and occupation meant relegating the colonized into a third zone between subjecthood and objecthood" (Mbembe 2003, 26).

The bifurcation of white and non-white spaces is used to justify foreign rule and the beneficence of those distributing material assistance in a crisis. "Charity is often embedded in more hierarchical understandings of humanity, as part of the obligations those with resources and standing owe to those without" (Calhoun 2010, 35). Conveniently, the conditions set the stage for penning a recurring narrative: "Moral white people come from the rich world to care for those in backward, remote places" (ibid., 54). Such primitive places appear locally as well as overseas colonies. Blauner (1969, 396) described the African American ghetto as a *de facto* internal colony. Bullard (1993) extended this categorization to all communities where people of color dwell. These "racialized spaces" not only designate where people of color should live, or are to do so, they also prescribe the natural and environmental hazards to which non-whites are vulnerable (Ducre 2008, 66–67). However, with regards to Hurricane María and Puerto Rico, we are not talking about a de facto colony, but a de jure one.

Commonly citizenship is discussed in dichotomous terms: either one has it or not. Since 1917 all Puerto Ricans have been U.S. citizens. The classic narrative insists that those with American citizenship are united in a common ideological bond that surpasses any ethnic or racial barriers (Kallen 1998; Lipset 1990, 2003; Spalding 2009). Throughout history, nativists have challenged that assumption claiming that *bona fide* American-ness was limited to the Teutonic race in the ninettenth century, while their twentieth-century counterparts expanded the brotherhood to include non-Muslim whites (Buchanan 2011; Strong 2009; Whitney 2007). Breaking with both of those traditions are academics who see citizenship as a nested phenomenon. They suggest that civic citizenship rhetoric masks a profoundly ethnic core (Kaufmann 1999; Yack 1996). "Thus, in the real world of democracy, the choice very often may not be between the faithful implementation of 'All persons are created equal' and blatant group discrimination. It may be a choice between de facto discrimination under the guise of liberal constitutional principles and something resembling two-tiered democracy" (Peled 1992, 440).

The realities of political and social practices, as per the scholars articulating a nested citizenship thesis, pull us toward more nuanced and variegated forms of citizenship. Marshall's (1950, 10) classic work was unique in partitioning citizenship into distinct civil, political, and social components. American citizenship is not an undifferentiated whole, rather, it "comprises both universalist and exclusionary commitments" (Bosniak 2006, 81). While they carry the same passport, Puerto Ricans clearly had a different kind of U.S. citizenship (Barreto 2016; Barreto and Lozano 2017). While they hold "nominal citizenship," the most basic form, they lack its more complete counterpart—"civil citizenship" (Cott 1998, 1448). A century ago Congress deemed Puerto Ricans worthy of citizenship and a permanent relationship with the United States—something denied to the Filipinos who "ungratefully" resisted U.S. rule in an armed insurrection (Cabranes 1978, 490). The political discourse of the early twentieth century racialized both communities, but to varying degrees (Thompson 2010, 200). In the second decade of that century, Congress feared the possible development of a vibrant separatist movement in Puerto Rico along the lines of the Philippines. Naturalizing Puerto Ricans was a move designed to cut off that possibility (Barreto and Lozano 2016, 1006). To justify that citizenship Puerto Rican islanders were rhetorically whitened, but only to a degree. Although racially mixed, "Puerto Ricans were *white enough* to warrant citizenship," but not white enough to warrant full equality under statehood (ibid. emphasis in the original text). As Venator-Santiago (2001, 907) noted, "Puerto Rican citizenship is directly linked to a status of space that was in turn created by racist ideologies." Indeed, "the US response to Hurricane María proved beyond the shadow of a doubt that residents of Puerto Rico have never really been first-class citizens" (Morales 2019, 3). A bitter pills for Puerto Ricans to swallow, particularly for those who champion the statehood cause, is that many on the mainland see Puerto Ricans as *brown* (Barreto 2020, 68).

CONCLUSION

The Trump administration's response to Hurricane María invite us to critically examine the larger debate about citizenship and the quintessence of American national identity. Trump's response was consistent with the racialization of Puerto Ricans and designating them a people less worthy of immediate aid than their white, mainland fellow citizens. And this case is inseparable from a larger process of prioritizing government responses based on the relative quality of particular U.S. citizens. The universal hope entrenched in Emma Lazarus's poem is incompatible with the demonization of black and brown outsiders, coupled with the *othering* of American citizens whose phenotypical characteristics deviate from his Nordic ideal. More than any presidency in modern times Trump pries open the Pandora's Box of what lies inside the inner sanctum of that national identity. For him and his followers, national authenticity is limited to a particular set of U.S. citizens. Consequently, they feel that the government is entitled to respond differently to natural disasters based not only on the damage wrought and the lives overturned, but on the qualities that separate the *worthy* from the *undeserving*.

NOTES

1. Ironically, the bill's acronym—*promesa*—means "promise" in Spanish.
2. *Downes v. Bidwell*, 182 U.S. 244, 287 (1901).
3. Women, particularly white women with children, were deemed worthy. That status applied less so able-bodied men. Historically non-heterosexuals were excluded from the *worthy* category. However, Chasin (2000, 35–41, 125) contends that straight

society has improved its perception of gays and lesbians in direct proportion to their capacity to consume. This change in attitude is also connected with a stereotype: lesbians and gays are presumed white.

REFERENCES

Andrés, José, and Richard Wolffe. *We Fed an Island: The True Story of Rebuilding Puerto Rico, One Meal at a Time.* New York: HarperCollins, 2018.

Baker, Peter, and Caitlin Dickerson. "Trump Warns Storm-Ravaged Puerto Rico That Aid Won't Last 'Forever'." *New York Times*, October 12, 2017. https://www.nytimes.com/2017/10/12/us/politics/trump-warns-puerto-rico-weeks-after-storms-federal-help-cannot-stay-forever.html

Barreto, Amílcar A. *Vieques, the Navy, and Puerto Rican Politics.* Gainesville: University Press of Florida, 2002.

———. "American Identity, Congress and the Puerto Rico Statehood Debate." *Studies in Ethnicity and Nationalism* 16, no. 1 (2016): 100–117.

———. *The Politics of Language in Puerto Rico: Revisited.* Gainesville: University Press of Florida, 2020.

Barreto, Amílcar A., and Kyle Lozano. "Hierarchies of Belonging: Intersecting Race, Ethnicity, and Territoriality in the Construction of US Citizenship." *Citizenship Studies* 21, no. 8 (2017): 999–1014.

Barreto, Amílcar A., and Nicholas Napolio. "Bifurcating American Identity: Partisanship, Sexual Orientation, and the 2016 Presidential Election." *Politics, Groups and Identities* 8, no. 1 (2018): 143–159.

Ben-Porath, Eran N., and Lee K. Shaker. "News Images, Race, and Attribution in the Wake of Hurricane Katrina." *Journal of Communication* 60, no. 3 (2010): 466–490.

Blauner, Robert. "Internal Colonialism and Ghetto Revolt." *Social Problems* 16, no. 4 (1969): 393–408.

Bosniak, Linda. *The Citizen and the Alien: Dilemmas of Contemporary Membership.* Princeton, NJ: Princeton University Press, 2006.

Buchanan, Patrick. *Suicide of a Superpower: Will America Survive to 2025?* New York: St. Martin's Press, 2011.

Bullard, Robert D. "Anatomy of Environmental Racism and the Environmental Justice Movement." In *Confronting Environmental Racism: Voices from the Grassroots*, edited by Robert D. Bullard, 15–39. Boston: South End Press, 1993.

Bush, George W. *Decision Points.* New York: Crown Publishers, 2010.

Cabán, Pedro. "PROMESA, Puerto Rico and the American Empire." *Latino Studies* 16, no. 2 (2018): 1–24.

Cabranes, José A. "Citizenship and the American Empire: Notes on the Legislative History of the United States Citizenship of Puerto Rico." *University of Pennsylvania Law Review* 127, no. 2 (1978): 391–492.

Calhoun, Craig. "The Idea of Emergency: Humanitarian Action and Global (Dis) Order." In *Contemporary States of Emergency: The Politics of Military and*

Humanitarian Interventions, edited by Didier Fassin and Mariella Pandolfi, 29–58. New York: Zone Books, 2010.

Chasin, Alexandra. *Selling Out: The Gay and Lesbian Movement Goes to Market.* New York: St. Martin's Press, 2000.

Colón Dávila, Javier. "¿Por qué no llevaron a Trump a ver los estragos de Loíza?" *El Nuevo Día*, San Juan, Puerto Rico, October 3, 2017. https://www.elnuevodia.com/noticias/locales/nota/porquenollevaronatrumpaverlosestragosenloiza-2362899/

Costa, Dennis. "Trump Compares Puerto Rico's Death Toll to Katrina's." *El Nuevo Día*, San Juan, Puerto Rico, October 3, 2017. https://www.elnuevodia.com/english/english/nota/trumpcomparespuertoricosdeathtolltokatrinas-2362763/

Dauber, Michele L. "The Sympathetic State." *Law and History Review* 23, no. 2 (2005): 387–442.

De Genova, Nicholas, and Ana Y. Ramos-Zayas. "Latino Rehearsals: Racialization and the Politics of Citizenship Between Mexicans and Puerto Ricans in Chicago." *Journal of Latin American Anthropology* 8, no. 2 (2003): 18–57.

Delgado, José A. "Donald Trump cuestiona el liderato de Carmen Yulín Cruz." *El Nuevo Día*, San Juan, Puerto Rico, September 30, 2017. https://www.elnuevodia.com/noticias/politica/nota/donaldtrumpcuestionaellideratodecarmenyulincruz-2361864/

"Donald Trump rechaza la estadidad para Puerto Rico." *El Nuevo Día*, San Juan, Puerto Rico, September 24, 2018. https://www.elnuevodia.com/noticias/eeuu/nota/donaldtrumprechazalaestadidadparapuertorico-2449034/

Ducre, K. Animashaun. "Hurricane Katrina as an Elaboration on an Ongoing Theme: Racialized Spaces in Louisiana." In *Seeking Higher Ground: The Hurricane Katrina Crisis, Race, and Public Policy Reader*, edited by Manning Marable and Kristen Clarke, 65–74. New York: Palgrave Macmillan, 2008.

Dyson, Michael E. *Come Hell or High Water: Hurricane Katrina and the Color of Disaster.* New York: Basic Civitas, 2005.

Essary, Elizabeth Helen, and Christian Ferney. "Pomp and Power, Performers and Politicians: The California Theatre State." *American Journal of Cultural Sociology* 1, no. 1 (2013): 96–124.

Feliciano, Zaida M. "IRS Section 936 and the Decline of Puerto Rico's Manufacturing." *Centro Journal* 30, no. 3 (2019): 30–42.

FEMA. "Hurricane Pam Exercise Concludes." Release Number: R6-04-093, July 23, 2004. https://www.fema.gov/news-release/2004/07/23/hurricane-pam-exercise-concludes

Ferré-Sadurní, Luis, and Anemona Hartocollis. "Maria Strikes, and Puerto Rico Goes Dark." *New York Times*, September 20, 2017. https://www.nytimes.com/2017/09/20/us/hurricane-maria-puerto-rico-power.html

Fiske, John. *Media Matters: Race and Gender in U.S. Politics.* Minneapolis: University of Minnesota Press, 1996.

Foucault, Michel. *Power/Knowledge: Selected Interviews & Other Writings, 1972–1977*, edited by Colin Gordon. New York: Vintage Books, 1980.

———. *Discipline & Punish: The Birth of the Prison*, translated by Alan Sheridan. New York: Vintage Books, 1995.

————. *"Society Must Be Defended": Lectures at the Collège de France, 1975–1976*, edited by Mauro Bertani and Alessandro Fontana, translated by David Macey. New York: Picador, 2003.

Gabriel, John. *Whitewash: Racialized Politics and the Media*. London: Routledge, 1998.

Gilens, Martin. "'Race Coding' and White Opposition to Welfare." *American Political Science Review* 90, no. 3 (1996): 593–604.

Giroux, Henry A. "Violence, Katrina, and the Biopolitics of Disposability." *Theory, Culture & Society* 24, nos. 7–8 (2007): 305–309.

Goldberg, David Theo. *The Racial State*. Malden, MA: Blackwell, 2002.

Gordon, Linda. "Who Deserves Help? Who Must Provide?" *The Annals of the American Academy of Political and Social Science* 577 (2001): 12–25.

Grosfoguel, Ramón. *Colonial Subjects: Puerto Ricans in a Global Perspective*. Berkeley: University of California Press, 2003.

Haney-López, Ian. *Dog Whistle Politics: How Coded Racial Appeals Have Reinvented Racism & Wrecked the Middle Class*. New York: Oxford University Press, 2014.

"Here's Donald Trump's Presidential Announcement Speech." *Time*, June 16, 2015. http://time.com/3923128/donald-trump-announcement-speech/

"Hillary Clinton pide a Trump que envié la Marina de Guerra a Puerto Rico." *El Nuevo Día*, San Juan, Puerto Rico, September 24, 2017. https://www.elnuevodia.com/noticias/eeuu/nota/hillaryclintonpideatrumpqueenvielamarinadeguerraapuertorico-2360061/

"How to Save Puerto Rico." Editorial. *New York Times*, May 31, 2016. https://www.nytimes.com/2016/05/31/opinion/what-may-be-puerto-ricos-best-hope.html

"Jorge Ramos critica la respuesta de Trump a la situación de la isla." *El Nuevo Día*, San Juan, Puerto Rico, September 28, 2017. https://www.elnuevodia.com/entretenimiento/farandula/nota/jorgeramoscriticalarespuestadetrumpalasituaciondelaisla-2361516/

Kallen, Horace. *Culture and Democracy in the United States*. New Brunswick, NJ: Transaction, 1998.

Katznelson, Ira. *When Affirmative Action Was White: An Untold Story of Racial Inequality in Twentieth-Century America*. New York: W. W. Norton, 2005.

Kaufmann, Eric. "American Exceptionalism Reconsidered: Anglo-Saxon Ethnogenesis in the 'Universal' Nation, 1776–1850." *Journal of American Studies* 33, no. 3 (1999): 437–457.

Kishore, Nishant, et al. "Morality in Puerto Rico After Hurricane Maria." *The New England Journal of Medicine*, 2018. https://www.nejm.org/doi/full/10.1056/NEJMsa1803972

Kroll-Smith, Steve, and Shelly Brown-Jeffy. "A Tale of Two American Cities: Disaster, Class and Citizenship in San Francisco, 1906 and New Orleans 2005." *Journal of Historical Sociology* 26, no. 4 (2013): 527–551.

Landis, Michele L. "Fate, Responsibility, and 'Natural' Disaster Relief: Narrating the American Welfare State." *Law & Society Review* 33, no. 2 (1999): 257–318.

Landler, Mark. "Trump Lobs Praise, and Paper Towels, to Puerto Rico Storm Victims." *New York Times*, October 3, 2017. https://www.nytimes.com/2017/10/03/us/puerto-rico-trump-hurricane.html

Levin, Josh. *The Queen: The Forgotten Life Behind an American Myth*. New York: Little, Brown and Co., 2019.

Lipset, Seymour M. *Continental Divide: The Values and Institutions of the United States and Canada*. London: Routledge, 1990.

———. *The First New Nation: The United States in Historical and Comparative Perspective*. New Brunswick, NJ: Transaction, 2003.

Lundskow, George. "Authoritarianism and Destructiveness in the Tea Party Movement." *Critical Sociology* 38, no. 4 (2012): 529–547.

Marable, Manning. "Seeking Higher Ground: Race, Public Policy and the Hurricane Katrina Crisis." In *Seeking Higher Ground: The Hurricane Katrina Crisis, Race, and Public Policy Reader*, edited by Manning Marable and Kristen Clarke, ix–xvi. New York: Palgrave Macmillan, 2008.

Marshall, Thomas H. *Citizenship and Social Class and Other Essays*. Cambridge: Cambridge University Press, 1950.

Maskovsky, Jeff. "Toward the Anthropology of White Nationalist Postracialism." *HAU: Journal of Ethnographic Theory* 7, no. 1 (2017): 433–440.

Mbembe, Achille. "Necropolitics." *Public Culture* 15, no. 1 (2003): 11–40.

Meléndez, Edwin. "The Politics of PROMESA." *Centro Journal* 30, no. 3 (2018): 43–71.

Molina-Guzmán, Isabel. "The Gendered Racialization of Puerto Ricans in TV News Coverage of Hurricane Maria." In *Journalism, Gender & Power*, edited by Cynthia Carter, Linda Steiner, and Stuart Allan, 331–346. New York: Routledge, 2019.

Morales, Ed. *Fantasy Island: Colonialism, Exploitation, and the Betrayal of Puerto Rico*. New York: Bold Type Press, 2019.

Morning Consult. "National Tracking Poll #170916." September 22–24, 2017. https://morningconsult.com/wp-content/uploads/2017/10/170916_crosstabs_pr_v1_KD.pdf

Negrón-Muntaner, Frances. "Our Fellow Americans: Why Calling Puerto Ricans "Americans" Will Not Save Them." In *Aftershocks of Disaster: Puerto Rico Before and After the Storm*, edited by Yarimar Bonilla and Marisol LeBrón, 113–123. Chicago: Haymarket Books, 2019.

Nix-Stevenson, Dara N. "A Query into the Social Construction of (Un)Natural Disasters: Teaching (About) the Biopolitics of Disposability." Ph.D. diss., University of North Carolina, Greensboro, 2013.

Olson, Joel. *The Abolition of White Democracy*. Minneapolis: University of Minnesota Press, 2004.

Pacheco Álvarez, Istra. "Visita relámpago de Donald Trump a iglesia en Guaynabo." *El Nuevo Día*, San Juan Puerto Rico, October 3, 2017. https://www.elnuevodia.com/noticias/locales/nota/visitarelampagodedonaldtrumpaiglesiaenguaynabo-2362884/

Peled, Yoav. "Ethnic Democracy and the Legal Construction of Citizenship: Arab Citizens of the Jewish State." *American Political Science Review* 86, no. 2 (1992): 432–443.

"Puerto Rico Deserves Better." Editorial. *New York Times*, September 28, 2017. https://www.nytimes.com/2017/09/28/opinion/puerto-rico-trump-hurricane-recovery.html

"Puerto Rico Is American. We Can't Ignore It Now." Editorial. *New York Times*, September 24, 2017. https://www.nytimes.com/2017/09/24/opinion/editorials/puerto-rico-maria-hurricane.html

Rivera Cedeño, Jomar J. "Carmen Yulín: 'Lo que hay es hambre, sed y desesperanza en este país'." *El Nuevo Día*, San Juan, Puerto Rico, September 29, 2017. https://www.elnuevodia.com/noticias/locales/nota/carmenyulinloquehayeshambresedydesesperanzaenestepais-2361741/

Robles, Frances, Lizette Alvarez, and Nicholas, Fandos. "In Battered Puerto Rico, Governor Warns of a Humanitarian Crisis." *New York Times*, September 25, 2017. https://www.nytimes.com/2017/09/25/us/puerto-rico-maria-fema-disaster-.html

Spalding, Matthew. *We Still Hold These Truths: Rediscovering Our Principles, Reclaiming Our Future*. Wilmington, DE: Intercollegiate Studies Institute, 2009.

Sterett, Susan M. "Need and Citizenship After Disaster." *Natural Hazards Review* 13, no. 3 (2012): 233–245.

Strong, Josiah. *Our Country: Its Possible Future and Its Present Crisis*. Charleston, SC: BiblioLife, 2009.

Sullivan, Laura. "How Puerto Rico's Debt Created A Perfect Storm Before The Storm." *NPR*, May 2, 2018. https://www.npr.org/2018/05/02/607032585/how-puerto-ricos-debt-created-a-perfect-storm-before-the-storm

Thompson, Lanny. *Imperial Archipelago: Representation and Rule in the Insular Territories Under U.S. Dominion After 1898*. Honolulu: University of Hawai'i, 2010.

Tierney, Kathleen, Christine Bevc, and Erica Kuligowski. "Metaphors Matter: Disaster Myths, Media Frames, and Their Consequences in Hurricane Katrina." *The Annals of the American Academy of Political and Social Science* 604, no. 1 (2006): 57–81.

Venator-Santiago, Charles R. "Race, Space, and the Puerto Rican Citizenship." *Denver University Law Review* 78 (2001): 907–919.

Victor, Daniel. "San Juan Mayor on Hurricane Response: 'This Is Not a Good News Story'." *New York Times*, September 29, 2017. https://www.nytimes.com/2017/09/29/us/san-juan-mayor.html

Vinik, Danny. "How Trump Favored Texas Over Puerto Rico." *Politico*, March 27, 2018. https://www.politico.com/story/2018/03/27/donald-trump-fema-hurricane-maria-response-480557

Weisskoff, Richard. *Factories and Food Stamps: The Puerto Rican Model of Development*. Baltimore, MD: Johns Hopkins University Press, 1985.

Whitney, Thomas. *A Defense of the American Policy, as Opposed to the Encroachments of Foreign Influence*. Whitefish, MT: Kessinger, 2007.

Yack, Bernard. "The Myth of the Civic Nation." *Critical Review* 10, no. 2 (1996): 193–211.

Chapter 5

"I Think They Capitalized . . . on a Lot of People's Loss"

Perceptions of Reconstruction after the Tuscaloosa Tornado

Ariane Prohaska

An EF-4 tornado killed fifty-three people and injured hundreds in Tuscaloosa County, Alabama, on April 27, 2011 (City of Tuscaloosa 2011). The storm caused significant damage and destruction of property, with 5,144 of the 6,850 homes in the tornado's path deemed destroyed or damaged (ACRE 2012). The neighborhoods most highly impacted by the event were those with higher percentages of low-income, minority residents (City of Tuscaloosa 2011).

There have been some studies assessing how the tornado impacted the behaviors of Tuscaloosa residents (Senkbeil et al. 2012, 2014; Stokes and Senkbeil 2016), but there has not yet been research examining residents' perceptions of the rebuilding and reconstruction process after this event, and survivors' perceptions of the reconstruction process is rarely studied at all. It is pertinent to study how those impacted by a natural disaster feel about the recovery of their city and/or neighborhood for a few reasons. First, research has revealed that resident involvement in recovery leads to higher satisfaction with the process and results of the process (e.g., Dias et al. 2016; Rand et al. 2011; Davidson et al. 2007). In turn, a few studies have shown that satisfaction with the recovery process is related to positive mental health outcomes (Huang and Wong 2013).

The voices often silenced in the reconstruction phase of a natural disaster are the people who are the most vulnerable before and immediately after the event. Community vulnerability perspective (Van Zandt et al. 2012) states that neighborhoods with fewer resources before a disaster recover more slowly that their resource-rich counterparts, which magnifies the impact of the event on neighborhood residents. Related, the social vulnerability perspective purports that gender, socioeconomic status, race, ethnicity, and age, among other statuses, affect individuals' capacity to prepare for and recover from natural disasters (Phillips and Fordham 2010; Bolin 2006; Morrow 1999; Blaikie et al. 1994). According to this perspective, the interaction between social and political systems produces differing levels of risk for being a victim of a disaster and divergent levels of recovery in its aftermath (e.g., Phillips and Fordham 2010; Blaikie et al. 1994). Having a low income (e.g., Van Zandt et al. 2012; Phillips and Fordham 2010; Peacock et al. 2007; Powers 2006; Fothergill and Peek 2004; Peacock and Girard 1997) and/or being a person of color (e.g., Van Zandt et al. 2012; Phillips and Fordham 2010; Bullard et al. 2009; Peacock et al. 2007; Peacock and Girard 1997) leads to less preparedness for a natural disaster and greater negative outcomes after the event. Similarly, community vulnerability perspective (Van Zandt et al. 2012) stresses that the most vulnerable neighborhoods will recover at a slower pace, resulting in adverse outcomes for residents of those areas. Since negative consequences associated with a disaster can happen to all residents, it is important to understand how survivors feel about their community's handling of the reconstruction process, and if these concerns are more pronounced for individuals of marginalized statuses.

Currently, little research exists that explains how individuals who experienced the tornado feel about the long-term rebuilding and recovery, particular in the unique case of a college town, where the economy is highly dependent on the university. Although people from marginalized groups experience the hardest impacts of natural disasters, they are not usually viewed as key stakeholders in the rebuilding process (Khunwishit and McEntire 2012). This lack of involvement in reconstruction may result in marginalized community members having negative opinions about the recovery process. This case study of Tuscaloosa, Alabama tornado survivors reveals regardless of social status, all participants have at least some negative perceptions of reconstruction, but the reasons for their negative attitudes vary by class, race, and ethnicity. This research reveals the importance of studying perceptions of the reconstruction process in connection to both involvement in recovery planning and long-term mental health outcomes after a disaster.

LITERATURE REVIEW

Previous research has consistently connected community input to greater satisfaction in the reconstruction process (e.g., Dias et al. 2016; Rand et al. 2011; Davidson et al. 2007). Satisfaction with reconstruction also depends on speed of the rebuilding process, which is related to levels of vulnerability; the most vulnerable populations before a natural disaster are the often the slowest to rebuild (e.g., Simmons and Sutter 2011; Finch et al. 2010; Bates and Green 2009; Morrow 1999; Bolin and Stanford 1991). Research on disaster survivors' perceptions of the reconstruction process is sparse, but can provide an explanatory bridge connecting community participation in reconstruction to long-term mental health outcomes of disaster survivors, particularly those who are the most socially vulnerable.

The research that exists on community perceptions of recovery does provide some useful information. Abramowitz (2005) studied six communities in Guinea that were victimized by Sierra Leonean and Liberian militaries from 2000 to 2001. Although individuals in all communities reported experiencing psychological distress, the communities that felt neglected by their governments and by nongovernmental organizations experienced higher levels of distress, or what he termed "collective trauma." Huang and Wong (2013) created a scale measuring impacted residents' satisfaction with governmental recovery after the 2018 Wenchaun earthquake, including items measuring satisfaction with: infrastructure, income recovery, assistance provided to one's family, the planning needed for community recovery, the fairness of resource distribution, openness and transparency of disaster recovery information, government respect of public opinion, public participation in planning and implantation of recovery, and overall satisfaction with recovery (425). Respondents reported about average levels of satisfaction with the government's recovery process and implementation. In addition, higher levels of satisfaction with recovery were associated with higher levels of life satisfaction.

Although this research highlights the importance of measuring satisfaction of the recovery process, no research has addressed satisfaction with recovery from a qualitative perspective in the United States. Although research has asked participants to identify problems with the reconstruction of their communities, the reasons why they feel dissatisfaction have been overlooked. It is expected that marginalized tornado survivors will have unique perspectives on how individuals perceive the local government's role. This chapter addresses this gap in the research.

METHOD

Participants

The data for this study was drawn from a larger study on economic and psychosocial stressors of tornado survivors in the long-term aftermath of the Tuscaloosa tornado between October 2014 and October 2016, interviews were conducted with twenty-nine individuals who had been directly impacted by the April 2011 Tuscaloosa tornado. Direct impact was defined as living in or being located in the path of the tornado when it struck, or having lost a loved one as a result of the storm. Several strategies were utilized in order to recruit a diverse group of participants. First, two Hispanic community groups were contacted via email and asked to share information about the study to members. Next, approximately eighteen churches in areas of the city with varying income levels and racial/ethnic compositions that were in the path of the storm were contacted by phone and email and asked to share the study flyer with congregants of the churches. These first two sampling methods were purposeful; individuals in poverty, who were displaced after the storm, and/or were undocumented immigrants are hard to reach via other methods of sampling (e.g., Creswell 2013). A Facebook page for tornado survivors was also created in order to recruit participants in the Tuscaloosa community. Finally and perhaps most importantly, study participants were asked to recommend other tornado survivors who may be interested in being a part of the study. As an incentive, participants received a $20 gift card to a local department store. Because of the sensitive nature of the interview, participants received information about mental health resources in the community before consenting to the study.

Interview

Tornado survivors participated in in-depth, semi-structured interviews. The PI trained three research assistants to about how to conduct interviews, which included mock interview training sessions. The PI was present for the first interview with each research assistants. Two of the research assistants were bilingual and interviewed the Spanish-speaking participants. The PI was present at each interview with Spanish-speaking participants so research assistants could summarize responses after each question, and assisted with probing for more information when necessary.

During the interviews, participants were asked questions about their pre-storm personal, financial, and employment histories. Second, interviewers asked about the day of the storm and the immediate aftermath, including questions about their experiences of the storm, if they or their loved ones experienced injuries and/or displacement, and how they were dealing with the emotional effects of the storm. Third, interviewers asked participants about their lives one year after the storm, including whether or not they had recovered emotionally and financially. Last, participants answered questions about their current lives, approximately four to five years after the storm, to find out if they believed their lives were better, worse, or the same following the storm. By asking these questions, interviewers could assess the impact of the storm on the survivors and whether or not participants have fully recovered emotionally and financially. Bilingual interviewers translated interviews from Spanish to English during transcription.

Analyses

QSR-NVivo data analysis software was used to organize and code the interviews using a grounded theory approach (Glaser and Strauss 1967). During transcription, notes were created about initial patterns in the data, and the transcripts were read and analyzed multiple times until the final coding categories emerged. In this paper, the analysis is focused on themes related to recovery and reconstruction problems that participants attributed to the city government, neighborhood changes, and/or shifts in community demographics. Although interviews did not specifically ask about perceptions of the reconstruction process, about a third of the sample used their interviews to discuss in detail their complaints about the recovery and reconstruction process, and three themes about recovery and reconstruction emerged: dissatisfaction with the city's response, frustration with the speed of the rebuilding of the city, and unhappiness with changes to the city landscape. Differences in perceptions of recovery by social class, race, and ethnicity are also discussed.

RESULTS AND DISCUSSION

Sample Characteristics

In order to describe the sample, demographic information was gathered from the twenty-nine interviewees. The participants in this study were racially diverse, including ten non-Hispanic white (34.5%), eight African American (27.6%), ten Hispanic (34.5%), and one Asian American (3.4%). The modal category for education was less than high school ($n = 8$, 27.6%), but 55.2 % of the participants had at least some college. The median income was $2000.00/ month (standard deviation = 3338.26). The median age of respondents was 41 years old, and most ($n = 23$, 79.3 %) of the participants were employed. Most of the participants were married ($n = 17$, 58.6%), had children ($n = 23$, 79.3%), and were women ($n = 24$, 84%)

The ten participants who discussed community recovery issues were racially and economically diverse. There were some differences between middle-class and lower-class individuals in their specific complaints, which will be explained below. The most common complaints can be classified into three broad themes. First, respondents mentioned that the city was not helpful to individuals in the recovery phase (thirteen instances mentioned by eight respondents). Second, participants voiced dissatisfaction with community changes (nine instances mentioned by six respondents). Four respondents were unhappy with the slow progress of the reconstruction of the city. These themes are discussed in detail below.

Underwhelming City Response

Individuals who discussed being unhappy with the city's response to recovery and reconstruction cited a variety of reasons for their dissatisfaction. Middle-class homeowners discussed the new codes and zoning laws that they believe were inconsistently applied during the rebuilding process. For example, Trudy, a sixty-year-old white, middle-class homeowner, had a disagreement about building back her home because of changes in the distance that a home could be from the road (or setbacks). After being told she had to move the placement of her house on her lot to adhere to the regulations on setbacks, she "researched the laws . . . and because my house is on a curve, I claimed it was a corner, which means my setbacks are different, and I built that house back as close to every little point I could." Another white middle-class home-owner, Jill, 48, mentioned that she and her husband "have come very in tune to the city council and codes and rebuilds and we saw some inconsistencies in some things that didn't make us happy. I mean multiple times my husband, he had to keep up and let his voice be heard at the city council meeting on the things that were going to affect us somewhere down the line."

Jill also mentioned the Tuscaloosa Forward plan (City of Tuscaloosa 2011). Tuscaloosa Forward was a plan for the reconstruction of Tuscaloosa that was created as the result of the work of city and community leaders, taking into account resident's input from a town hall meeting (with 300 participants) and online comments from residents. The resulting document contained a plan focusing on seven "big ideas" for the future of the city: (1) a "path of remembrance and revitalization, a green space with walking paths throughout the path of the tornado; (2) connected neighborhoods via walkways, sidewalks, and improved transit; (3) village centers, or areas within neighborhoods where activities, services, and amenities are located; (4) coordinated facilities and public uses, e.g., where schools, recreation, and other services can be concentrated; (5) model neighborhoods that involve rebuilding in ways that integrate within the existing neighborhood and across neighborhoods; (6) revitalize main corridors where economic and social needs were previously met; and (7) respecting the uniqueness of the distinct districts in the city.

Although the public participated in the formation of Tuscaloosa Forward and there was general satisfaction with the plan at its inception, after reconstruction began, opinions of how well the city was adhering to the plan varied. For example, according to Jill, the house across the street that was quickly built for the purpose of being rented by college students did not follow the stipulations set forth by the Tuscaloosa Forward Plan, namely one of the visions that stated that the rebuilt houses would include " well-designed homes that are durable, healthy, efficient, and green" (13). Said Jill: "and that just really devalues my house."

Lower-income tornado survivors who rented or owned mobile homes, on the other hand, highlighted their distrust of city officials over the use of money that they believe should have helped those less fortunate. For example, Ann, a fifty-five-year-old African American woman on SSI wondered "what are they doing with all this money and the gifts? Who hiding, who holding that? They need to start sending us a check." Abigail, a fifty-one-year-old African American woman on public assistance, wondered why the hardest hit and slowest to rebuild neighborhood, Alberta City (Weber and Lichtenstein 2017) did not have a storm shelter when others were being built around Tuscaloosa County, stating "everybody have a storm shelter but we don't have a storm shelter down there in Alberta City." Although she was mistaken (a storm shelter is located in a school in this neighborhood), her response points out the importance of disseminating knowledge about tornado safety to hard-to-reach people, including low-income or unemployed individuals who have may not have access to the internet or other sources of information (e.g., Phillips and Morrow 2007). These findings echo the rebuilding process in post-Katrina New Orleans, where competition for scarce resources and poor communication from government officials resulted in inequitable rebuilding process, exacerbating pre-existing community vulnerabilities (Brand and Seidman 2008).

One final complaint about the city was related to distrust surrounding a "papers" law enacted by the state of Alabama in 2011. Previous to the April 27, 2011, tornado, Alabama passed the Beason-Hammon Alabama Taxpayer and Citizen Protections Act or H.B. 56 (Alabama State Legislature 2011), which required law enforcement to ask individuals who may have committed crimes and are assumed to be undocumented for proof of their legal status in the United States. If the suspect did not carry their papers, the law demanded that they be arrested. The law also denied undocumented immigrants any public services (e.g., public school), and business owners could be prosecuted for knowingly employing undocumented workers. The existence of this law, scheduled to be enforced in June 2011, led many Hispanic tornado survivors to distrust city leaders and law enforcement after the tornado. For example, a Hispanic woman mentioned a conversation that the mayor had with members of her church:

He said, "there is a law that passed here in Alabama, but you all please don't worry. Right now we all have the same color of blood." . . . And they said, "Go get help. Please, report crimes," because there were already people being robbed, but they wouldn't talk to the police out of fear. So, uh, the Mexican consulate came, too, and other consulates, to help and all that. But I will tell you, that wasn't enough.

Although the mayor was not a proponent of H.B. 56, trust in both city leaders and law enforcement was already eroded. The same woman also discussed how the law led to people leaving the state after the tornado without informing law enforcement, stating "the city was ugly, and the law came that said that undocumented people couldn't be here. They left to Chicago. They did leave." This was echoed by another woman who said she had coworkers who "were very affected" and "left the state afterwards. They went to Texas." The disappearance of Hispanic community members after the tornado not only caused Hispanic community members to lose social support, necessary for economic and psychological recovery (e.g., Kaniasty and Norris 1993), but likely resulted in inaccurate counting of missing persons and perhaps the number of individuals who were killed or injured by the tornado, which is important to emergency managers who seek to mitigate future negative disaster outcomes. Another Hispanic woman mentioned "the Hispanic community didn't have many voices that were heard." Fellow tornado survivors attributed this to the focus on college students in the rebuild of Tuscaloosa.

Dissatisfaction with Community and Neighborhood Changes

Changes in the landscape and content of neighborhoods were mentioned by participants. Among the problems mentioned was the building of new, high-end student apartments. Tornado survivors saw the University of Alabama students, and perhaps the university itself, infringing on neighborhoods once occupied mostly by non-students. These apartments were not only replacing less expensive housing complexes, but also supplanting lower-income rental housing in Alberta City, leaving respondents to wonder where people were moving. Trudy expressed anger toward the city of Tuscaloosa, asserting "it's very hard to say and I'm very angry about it, because so many people were lower income and one of the damn things they have not done . . . in this town is to create affordable housing." Darren, an African American schoolteacher, stated, "I grew up in Alberta too so that's freaking me out and so, it was nothing! And people we knew, 'cause we knew people that lived there and we're wondering and you know, their houses are gone and we're like where is everybody?" Discussing the rebuilding of a Baptist church in Alberta, Ann believed that the church was advertising to a mostly white clientele. She discussed the existence of a women's group that was held on the church's damaged grounds before the reconstruction of a bigger, more modern church in the neighborhood:

And after that we went in the little yellow house they had, okay? We women was there every Thursday, okay. And then they turned around and had a women's and men's group. Okay, all the groups, they stopped with us, with all us black-I didn't say that- all of us got excluded out. So what does that tell you? So basically, let me just express myself, be myself, because it's more black right around that church. And now you can count the blacks that go, and that may be seven people when there should be 40, 50, okay?

Ann was asserting that the construction of a new church resulted in church leaders recruiting a whiter, perhaps wealthier, clientele and leaving black community members without its previous spiritual community.

As a result of both the tornado and the increase in enrollment at the University of Alabama (for more, see Smart and Prohaska 2017), both low-income and middle-income tornado survivors mentioned the fear of gentrification. Trudy declared, "our biggest concern is Alberta is gonna be gentrified." She continued, "they're gonna upscale this place and, which is fine for my property value, but that's not morally where I am. Where I am is where do these people live and what are you going to do for them?" Darren expressed anger at the University of Alabama as well as the city of Tuscaloosa, arguing "I think they capitalized, to me, or tried to capitalize on a lot of people's loss and how they're spreading out into Alberta and to build the new road or whatever and buying people's houses and displacing them I guess." He later stated, "now some of the new business and whatnot are cool. I think we have too many apartments um, for some reason as soon as we got through the tornado now we have apartments everywhere." Individuals who lived in the community pre-storm and continued to live there during the reconstruction phase were unhappy about the neglect of longtime residents in comparison to the temporary students. These statements reflect "place attachment" (Norris et al. 2008), or the emotional connection individuals feel toward their city or neighborhood that are important to one's self concept. Similar themes of place attachment were found by Barrios (2011) in his study of gentrification of post-Katrina Tremé, where longtime working-class, African American residents felt that the presence of new middle-class "outsiders" fundamentally changed the neighborhood. Those who are deeply rooted to communities that undergo considerable change in the aftermath of a natural disaster may experience longer and more pronounced negative outcomes if they feel that their voices are not heard by leaders in their community.

Slow Rebuild

The last major theme related to tornado survivors' frustrations with recovery and reconstruction in Tuscaloosa was the perceived (slow) speed of the

rebuilding process. Two respondents mentioned the emotional impact of seeing condemned houses and businesses remaining standing months after the
storm. Abigail discussed the year after the storm in Alberta City: "I guess they
were doing their best to clean up but you just had to walk around the debris
and stuff and stuff was still standing, was still down. They had knocked them
down but the debris and stuff was still standing, and that was like the middle
of the year 2012." Lisa discussed having to look at the damaged house across
the street. "We had like half empty houses that just collected wildlife, um,
which was bad because we got a lot of snakes and rats and stuff." She later
discussed how the damage resulted in "tornado tourism": "I mean I remember
specifically there was this church group that came through and had this big
old cross on the side of the van, and they got out and took a photo op in front
of this house across the street." This inability to return to normalcy has been
connected to slow emotional recovery (e.g., Bolin 1985).

In addition, lack of businesses in Alberta City five years after the storm
was concerning to two residents. Abigail was also concerned about the lack
of businesses in walking distance of her home in Alberta, stating "we don't
have that many stores and there's some businesses coming back in Alberta
City and there's some they said isn't gonna come back and I feel that, I hate
to say it, but I feel like they kind of been draggin' on building Alberta City
back up, ya know?" Still four years after the storm, the Tuscaloosa Forward
plan to create village centers for shopping and entertainment had not been
implemented and was affecting individuals without transportation.

CONCLUSION

Although research has look consistently at how vulnerability affects the
recovery from disasters, and how involvement of the most vulnerable in
the recovery and reconstruction phases affects community satisfaction with
the rebuilding of communities, there has been little research on community
perceptions of the rebuilding process. As Huang and Wong (2013) revealed,
community satisfaction with the reconstruction process is related to life satisfaction, which is critical for residents wishing to return to normalcy after a
natural disaster. Researchers must not only ask about satisfaction with recovery, but investigate the reasons that individuals are upset with the reconstruction of their communities. Ignoring disaster survivors' perceptions recovery
may lead to misjudging community and individual resilience.

This research reveals that five years after the tornado, vulnerable individuals
in marginalized communities expressed the most discord with the rebuilding of
Tuscaloosa. Many of the participants in this disaster recovery study, from different social statuses and with differing ties to their Tuscaloosa neighborhoods,

voiced criticism of the reconstruction process. As this was a qualitative study, the original goal was to gather detailed information about tornado survivors' psychological and economic well-being about five years after the tornado. Participants' perceptions of being ignored during the reconstruction process, along with the reasons they were unhappy with the new, altered landscape of the city, emerged from these interviews. Whereas middle-class tornado survivors worried about the changing city landscape and building codes, individuals of lower incomes and people of color felt distrust toward city officials.

These findings reflect the main tenets of the social vulnerability and community vulnerability perspectives. Well-situated individuals are mostly concerned with bouncing back to their pre-storm economic status, and any impediments to their return to normalcy caused these residents stress. On the other hand, marginalized survivors were concerned with their survival; these participants were struggling to get back on their feet, and felt that the slow rebuilding of their communities was hindering their capacities to meet basic needs. Although research shows that regardless of social class, return to normalcy can positively affect emotional recovery (Bolin 1985), white and middle-class tornado survivors possessed resources before the storm, such as insured homes in neighborhoods with higher homeownership rates and higher incomes (Weber and Lichtenstein 2014), that were necessary to accelerate their emotional healing and to cope with permanent changes to the city's landscape.

Further, Hispanic tornado survivors were dealing with unique pre-storm vulnerabilities related to state immigration law and insecure employment. Although many of these tornado survivors had not been living in Tuscaloosa as long as non-Hispanic participants (and therefore experienced less place attachment), Hispanic survivors believed that returning to normalcy in Tuscaloosa was unlikely for them. For Hispanic disaster survivors, particularly undocumented workers, trust in government is crucial, but perhaps even less likely in the current political climate. For example, undocumented Houstonians who experienced Hurricane Harvey were skeptical of leaders who said they would not be reported to immigration officials if they pursued aid for their families (Sacchetti 2017). If distrust is presence pre-disaster, some individuals within a given community will not be able to bounce back, and a return to pre-storm inequities will likely follow.

This case study of Tuscaloosa, Alabama shows further support for social vulnerability and community vulnerability perspectives of disaster recovery. However, research conducted in the aftermath of disasters should examine the connections between satisfaction with the reconstruction process and long-term economic and psychological well-being. Without this information, we cannot assume neighborhood resilience is a reflection of individual resilience.

REFERENCES

Abramowitz, Sharon A. "The Poor Have Become Rich, and the Rich Have Become Poor: Collective Trauma in the Guinean Languette." *Social Science and Medicine* 61, no. 10 (2005): 2106–2118.

Barrios, Roberto E. "'If You Did Not Grow Up Here, You Cannot Appreciate Living Here': Neoliberalism, Spacetime, and Affect in Post-Katrina Recovery Planning." *Human Organization* 70, no. 2 (2011): 118–127.

Bates, Lisa K., and Rebekah A. Green. "Housing Recovery in the Ninth Ward: Disparities in Policy, Process, and Prospects." In *Race, Place, and Environmental Justice After Hurricane Katrina*, edited by Robert D. Bullard and Beverly Wright, 229–248. Boulder, Colorado: Westview Press, 2000.

Beason-Hammon Alabama Taxpayer and Citizen Protection Act, H.B. 56 (AL 2011).

Blaikie, Piers, Terry Cannon, Ian Davis, and Ben Wisner. *At Risk: Natural Hazards, People's Vulnerability and Disasters*. New York, NY: Routledge, 2014.

Bolin, Robert. "Disaster and Long-Term Recovery Policy: A Focus on Housing and Families." *Policy Studies Review* 4, no. 4 (1985): 709–715.

Bolin, Robert C. "Race, Class, Ethnicity, and Disaster Vulnerability." In *Handbook of Disaster Research*, edited by Havidan Rodriguez, Enrico L. Quarantelli, and Russell R. Dynes, 113–129. New York, NY: Springer Press, 2006.

Bolin, Robert C., and Lois Stanford. 1991. "Shelter, Housing, and Recovery: A Comparison of U.S. Disasters." *Disasters* 45, no. 1 (1991): 25–34.

Brand, Anna Olivia, and Karl Seidman. "Assessing Post-Katrina Recovery in New Orleans: Recommendations for Equitable Rebuilding." Department of Urban Studies and Planning, 2018. Accessed November 13, 2019. https://dusp.mit.edu/publication/assessing-post-katrina-recovery-new-orleans-recommendations-equitable-rebuilding

Bullard, Robert D., and Beverly Wright. *Race, Place, and Environmental Justice After Hurricane Katrina: Struggles to Reclaim, Rebuild and Revitalize New Orleans and the Gulf Coast*. Boulder, CO: Westview Press, 2009.

Cerdá, Magdalena, Magdalena Paczkowski, Sandro Galea, Kevin Nemethy, Claude Péan, and Moise Desvarieux. "Psychopathology in the Aftermath of the Haiti Earthquake: A Population-Based Study of Posttraumatic Stress Disorder and Major Depression." *Depression and Anxiety* 30, no. 5 (2013): 413–424.

Creswell, John W. *Qualitative Inquiry and Research Design: Choosing Among Five Approaches*. Thousand Oaks, CA: Sage, 2013.

Crowley, Sheila. "Where Is Home? Housing for Low-Income People After the 2005 Hurricanes." In *There is No Such Thing as a Natural Disaster: Race, Class and Hurricane Katrina*, edited by Chester Hartman and Gregory D. Squires, 121–166. New York, NY: Routledge, 2006.

David, Emmanuel, and Elaine Enarson. *The Women of Katrina: How Gender, Race, and Class Matter in an American Disaster*. Nashville, TN: Vanderbilt University Press, 2012.

Davidson, Colin H., Cassidy Johnson, Gonzalo Lizzaralde, Nese Dikman, and Alicia Sliwinski. "Truths and Myths about Community Participation in Post-Disaster Housing Projects." *Habitat International* 31, no. 1 (2007): 100–115.

Dias, Mahawattha, Kaushal Keraminiyage, and Kushani De Silva. "Post-Disaster Permanent Housing and Long-term Satisfaction of Post-disaster Resettled Communities: The Case of Post-Tsunami Sri Lanka." *International Journal of Disaster Prevention and Management* 25, no. 5 (2016): 581–594.

Finch, Christina, Christopher T. Emrich, and Susan L. Cutter. "Disaster Disparities and Differential Recovery in New Orleans." *Population and Environment* 31, no. 4 (2010): 179–202.

Fothergill, Alice, Enrique G. M. Maestas, and Joanna DeRouen Darlington. "Race, Ethnicity, and Disasters in the United States: A Review of the Literature." *Disasters* 23, no. 2 (1999): 156–173.

Fothergill, Alice, and Lori A. Peek. "Poverty and Disasters in the United States: A Review of Recent Sociological Findings." *Natural Hazards* 32 (2004): 89–110.

Girard, Chris, and Walter G. Peacock. "Ethnicity and Segregation: Post-Hurricane Relocation." In *Hurricane Andrew: Ethnicity, Gender and the Sociology of Disasters*, edited by W. G. Peacock, B. H. Morrow, and H. Gladwin, 191–205. New York: Routledge, 1997.

Gould, Charles W. "The Right to Housing Recovery After Natural Disasters." *Harvard Human Rights Journal* 22 (2009): 169–204.

Groen, Jeffrey A., and Anne E. Polivka. "Going Home After Hurricane Katrina: Determinants of Return Migration and Changes in Affected Areas." *Demography* 47, no. 4 (2010): 821–844.

Kaniasty, Krzysztof, and Fran H. Norris. "A Test of the Social Support Deterioration Modelin the Context of Natural Disaster." *Journal of Personality and Social Psychology* 64, no. 3 (1993): 395–408.

Khunwishit, Somporn, and David A. McEntire. "Testing Social Vulnerability Theory: A Quantitative Study of Hurricane Katrina's Perceived Impact on Residents Living in FEMA Designated Disaster Areas." *Journal of Homeland Security and Emergency Management* 9, no. 1 (2012): 1–16.

Morrow, Betty Hearn. "Identifying and Mapping Community Vulnerability." *Disasters* 23 (1999): 1–18.

Norris, Fran H., Susan P. Stevens, Betty Pfefferbaum, Karen F. Wyche, and Rose L. Pfefferbaum. "Community Resilience as a Metaphor, Theory, Set of Capacities, and Strategy for Disaster Readiness." *American Journal of Community Psychology* 41 (2007): 127–150.

Peacock, Walter Gillis, and Chris Girard. "Ethnic and Racial Inequalities in Hurricane Damage and Insurance Settlements." In *Hurricane Andrew: Ethnicity, Gender, and the Sociology of Disasters*, edited by Walter Gillis Peacock, Betty Hearn Morrow, and Hugh Gladwin, 171–179. New York, NY: Routledge, 1997.

Peacock, Walter Gillis, Nicole Dash, and Yang Zhang. "Shelter and Housing Recovery Following Disaster." In *Handbook of Disaster Research*, edited by Havidan Rodriguez, Enrico L. Quarentelli, and Russell R. Dynes, 258–274. New York, NY: Springer, 2007.

Phillips, Brenda D. "Cultural Diversity in Disasters: Sheltering, Housing, and Long-Term Recovery." *International Journal of Mass Emergencies and Disasters* 11, no. 1 (1993): 99–110.

Phillips, Brenda D., Deborah S. K. Thomas, Alice Fothergill, and Lynn Blinn-Pike. *Social Vulnerability to Disasters*. Boca Raton, FL: CRC Press, 2010.

Phillips, Brenda D., and Maureen Fordham. "Introduction." In *Social Vulnerability to Disasters*, edited by Brenda D. Phillips, Deborah S. K. Thomas, Alice Fothergill, and Lynn Blinn-Pike, 1–26. Boca Raton, FL: CRC Press, 2010.

Rand, Emily Christensen, Seki Hirano, and Ilan Kelman. "Post-Tsunami Housing Resident Satisfaction in Aceh." *International Development Planning Review* 33, no. 2 (2011): 188–211.

Sachetti, Maria. "For Houston's Many Undocumented Immigrants, Storm Is Just the Latest Challenge. *The Washington Post*, last modified August 28, 2017. https://www.washingtonpost.com/local/immigration/for-houstons-many-undocumented-immigrants-storm-is-just-the-latest-challenge/2017/08/28/210f5466-8c1d-11e7-84c0-02cc069f2c37_story.html?utm_term=.bbe5ff3bafa5

Senkbeil, Jason C., David A. Scott, Pilar Guinazu-Walker, and Meganne S. Rockman. "Ethnic and Racial Differences in Tornado Hazard Perception, Preparedness, and Lead Time in Tuscaloosa." *The Professional Geographer* 66, no. 4 (2016): 610–620.

Senkbeil, Jason C., Meganne S. Rockman, and John B. Mason. "Shelter Seeking Plans of Tuscaloosa Residents for a Future Tornado Event." *Weather, Climate, and Society* 4, no. 3 (2012): 159–171.

Simmons, Kevin M., and Daniel Sutter. *Economic and Societal Impacts of Tornadoes*. Boston, MA: American Meteorological Society, 2011.

Smart, Kasi, and Ariane Prohaska. "Disaster Capitalism, Housing Vulnerability, and the Tuscaloosa Tornado: A Critical Analysis of Rebuilding Efforts." *International Journal of Mass Emergencies and Disasters* 35, no. 1 (2017): 1–8.

Stokes, Courtney, and Jason C. Senkbeil. "Facebook and Twitter, Communication, Shelter, and the 2011 Tuscaloosa Tornado." *Disasters* 41, no. 1 (2016): 194–208.

"Tuscaloosa, Alabama Housing Needs Analysis." Alabama Center for Real Estate (ACRE). Accessed February 12, 2013.

"Tuscaloosa Forward." City of Tuscaloosa, Tuscaloosa, AL, last modified 2011. http://www.tuscaloosanews.com/assets/pdf/TL2315982.pdf

Van Zandt, Shannon, Walter Gillis Peacock, Dustin Henry, Himanshu Grover, Wesley E. Highfield, and Samuel D. Brody. "Mapping Social Vulnerability to Enhance Housing and Neighborhood Resilience." *Housing Policy Debate* 22, no. 1 (2012): 29–55.

Weber, Joe, and Bronwen Lichtenstein. "Building Back: Stratified Recovery After an EF-4 Tornado in Tuscaloosa, Alabama." *City and Community* 14, no. 2 (2015): 186–205.

Chapter 6

No Port in the Storm

Hurricanes and the Impact of Criminal Records

Pamela Ray Koch[1] and Dennis Feaster

"If you go to a shelter for #Irma and you have a warrant, we'll gladly escort you to the safe and secure shelter called the Polk County Jail." (Polk County Sheriff Twitter, Sept 6, 2017)

"If you go to a shelter for #Irma, be advised: Sworn LEOS will be at every shelter, checking Ids. Sex offenders/predators will not be allowed. (Polk County Sheriff Twitter, Sept 6, 2017)

As Hurricane Irma approached Florida in the fall of 2017, Polk County sheriff Grady Judd took to Twitter to advise residents how to protect themselves. While the country reeled from the devastation of Hurricane Harvey less than a month previously, the dangers of a category 5 storm were very apparent. That is why it was surprising when Sheriff Judd's Twitter feed stated that everyone with a warrant would be taken to county jail and that sex offenders would not be allowed in the county's hurricane shelters. This was compounded when the sheriff's spokeswoman, Carrie Horstman, clarified that nonviolent misdemeanor offenders would in fact be arrested if they went to shelters as law enforcement had an obligation, regardless of the rationale behind the warrant. The implication discouraged individuals who were behind on child support or had too many traffic violations from seeking appropriate shelter during a natural disaster. This decision seemingly resentenced many individuals and all sex offenders to potential death via hurricane for crimes that may have been committed decades ago, or perhaps were even process violations resulting in a warrant.

This essay examines the structural barriers that offenders in general and sex offenders specifically experience with re-entry in this era of mass incarceration in the United States. The collateral consequences of adjudication is not a new area of inquiry, however, linking this to the issue of disaster preparedness is, and is overdue. Further, we touch on the role intellectual disability plays intensifying the impacts of criminal during natural disasters.

MASS INCARCERATION AND CRIMINAL RECORDS IN AMERICA

It is no secret to social scientists that America has become more punitive in its criminal justice philosophy. The term mass incarceration is well understood by the scholarly community, the policy community and the lay public alike. This refers to the growth in arrests, as well as an increase in the incarceration rates in the United States since the 1970s. This growth coupled with the fact that the United States already led the world in incarceration has resulted in an explosion of our prison population as well as the population of individuals under community corrections, those with warrants and those who are those classified as felons and subjected to consequences long beyond their official sentences. Until early in the 1970s prison populations were stable for five decades at around 110 per 100,000 adults in population (Blumstein and Beck 1999; Visher and Travis 2003). However during the past thirty years of the twentieth century, the rate skyrocketed to 470 per 100,000 in population in 2000 and to 751 per 100,000 in 2005 representing a 600 percent increase in twenty-five years (Visher and Travis 2003).

Mandatory minimums, truth in sentencing, three-strike laws and other "get tough on crime" policies are responsible for much of the increased incarceration. These policies have also increased the number of people who are in community corrections with a 75 percent increase in probation and parole populations (Wynn 2012). In fact between 1980 and 2000, technical violations for parole increased sevenfold and 1/33 adults were under correctional supervision of one sort or another, up from 1/90 in 1980 (Travis and Lawrence 2002; Wynn 2012). The rise in incarceration rates has not spread its reach equally throughout the population. Black men have borne more than their fair share being seven times more likely than whites to have spent time in prison before their fortieth birthday (Western 2007). Finally, the rise in incarceration has led to a rise in another population—one that is not a form of supervision nor a criminal status: individuals undergoing re-entry or reintegration in society. Four times as many people are leaving prison in 2002 compared to twenty-five years ago which led the federal government to award $100 million for programs aimed at reintegrating formerly incarcerated individuals (Visher and Travis 2003).

Re-entry

For offenders leaving prison, the first priority is securing housing and this is often the most daunting task of reintegration. The ability to find quality affordable housing is of utmost importance (Bruce et al. 2014; Metraux and Culhane 2004). Up to 10 percent of offenders leave prison to homelessness, and many more have residential instability or go to nonsober homes which increase the likelihood of recidivism and 7 percent of shelter populations come from jails or prison (Curtin 2005). Communities that avoid housing needs of offenders in fact trade recidivism and lowered public safety (Bradley and Oliver 2001). Families of former offenders are also often reluctant to provide housing assistance to them (Curtin 2005). This is unfortunate given that returning to family roles creates identity and grounding that is positively correlated with reentry success (Sampson and Laub 1993; Uggen et al. 2003).

The community that an offender returns to is noted as an important feature of reintegration success (Visher and Travis 2003). Unfortunately, they also increasingly move back to neighborhoods that are marked by social disorganization which are densely populated and little sense of community (Travis et al. 2001; Clear et al. 2001). All of these factors are linked to rates of crime and recidivism (Sampson 2002). The goal for successful reintegration is collective efficacy in a community. Collective efficacy is defined as a commitment to the collective good and a sense of trust among community members; the same things that promote successful prisoner reentry also promote better disaster response as well, but have been elusive to returning offenders (Sampson et al. 1997).

Social networks and the connected social capital have been shown to play a large part in a successful reentry (Clear 2007; Farrall 2004). Coleman defined social capital as having two fundamental features: it consists of some aspect of social structure and facilitates certain actions of actors within the structure (Coleman 1988). These resources assist former offenders in gaining knowledge and opportunities, including knowledge of how to protect themselves (Taylor 2013). Those who have limited or only weak ties to their communities have fewer constraints to committing crime (Bahr et al. 2005) As former inmates build social capital and become attached to conventional aspects of community, they also develop a reason for conformity and have more to lose from recidivism (Carlson 2004; Hirschi 1969; Laub and Sampson 2001).

Many of those formerly incarcerated see these social resources diminish during incarceration, making tapping into them difficult during the best of times and potentially impossible when faced with a natural disaster (Roberts

2004; Clear 2007). Because the reentry period can be lonely and former offenders can lack these important social networks, they may turn to official sources as a surrogate social capital. If faced with Sheriff Judd's tweets, the results are potentially disastrous.

Natural Disasters as Part of Collateral Consequences

The social capital that reentry literature shows is necessary for successful reintegration is eroded by collateral consequences associated with a felony conviction (Whittle 2018). In general, after an offender attempts to reintegrate into a community they find that there are a host of rights and privileges that are elusive to them due to the collateral consequences of having justice system involvement in their history.

Originally known as "civil death" and later "civil disabilities" by English Courts, collateral consequences are the secondary impacts that hinder complete reintegration and serve as a continued (sometimes lifelong) punishment after an offender leaves prison. In essence they create barriers to civil life and blur the boundary between criminal and civil law (Mele and Miller 2005). These techniques are considered "collateral" by the justice system and are portioned from the direct consequences passed down by courts (Shanahan 2012). There is a strong history of the use of collateral consequences in western society in general (Miller and Spillane 2012). Collateral consequences are found throughout federal, state, and municipal codes and impact an estimated 1/50 adults in America on some level or another (Saxonhouse 2004). These penalties run the gamut from deportation, refusal of government benefits, loss of child custody, bans on federal financial aid, employment and licensing barriers, and loss of driving privileges and firearm possession, as well as the more well-known disenfranchisement of those convicted of a felony (Saxonhouse 2004; Shanahan 2012; Pinard 2009). These consequences bring decreased status and a social stigma that prevents successful reentry (LaFollette 2005).

Voting is regarded as a seminal aspect of civic participation. As such, for many felons the loss of the ability to vote poses a significant obstacle to reintegration (Miller and Spillane 2012). The right to vote is a symbol of a community stakeholder and many offenders list it as an important component to reentry (Whittle 2018; Solomon et al. 2001; Uggen et al. 2003). All states have some degree of felon disenfranchisement, highlighting the punitive attitude toward offenders. This prohibit individuals from participating in policy development that impacts them in meaningful ways, like barring them from seeking shelter during natural disasters.

Furthermore, these policies of disenfranchisement disproportionately impact people of color (Handelsman 2005). Similar to literacy tests and poll taxes, they are ostensibly race-neutral, but clearly have impacted Black and

Latino citizens more (Preuhs 2001; Hill 1994; Shapiro 1993). The policies were initially developed in the United States during Reconstruction—a time when Black suffrage was being legislated (Behrens et al. 2003). Between 1850 and 2002, states with the highest population of non-white citizens passed the most restrictive laws (Uggen and Manza 2004). For instance, in the late 1990s Utah and Massachusetts imposed more voting restrictions on felons, even as both states saw large increases in their minority populations prior to the passing these policies (Preuhs 2001).

Housing is a salient aspect of reintegration. It is also influenced by collateral consequences to a large degree. Many felons are barred from public housing (Curtin 2005). The picture is even more bleak in the private housing sector. Helfgott found that 67 percent of landlords inquire about criminal backgrounds. This, coupled with credit history checks, limited employment, and diminished job skills, make finding housing very difficult (Helfgott 1997; Roman 2004; Visher et al. 2006). Landlords fear being held responsible for the actions of the former offenders should they recidivate, and also worry about losing money to other tenants who may leave if they lease to offenders, particularly sexual offenders (Clark 2007). This reasoning in the community is likely similar to that of sheriffs who prohibit offenders' access to shelters during natural disasters; they fear that allowing equal protection to offenders will keep others from accessing essential resources. In this way, these consequences spill over into disaster preparation. After being denied housing and shelter care due to their criminal background, it is likely to influence the motivation to seek disaster shelter care. This is compounded when the sheriff is promoting that they may not be welcome there. For many in this position, it seems safer to try to weather the storm at home rather than being turned away once an individual finds a shelter.

The "civil death" of collateral consequences are often unknown until they impact the individual, with defendants very rarely informed of the consequences during a plea bargain or trial phase (Mele and Miller 2005). They are also implemented by the community in formal and informal ways (Whittle 2018). One of the informal ways that collateral consequences function is by making former offenders feel that they are not a legitimate part of the community, such as being told they are not welcome at life-preserving shelters. Collateral consequences have actually been linked to recidivism (Pager 2007; Harding et al. 2014; Mauer and Chesney-Lind 2002). Sohoni found that recidivism and public access to criminal records online are positively correlated, reinforcing the idea that the communities to which offenders return are of the utmost importance (Sohoni 2014; Whittle 2018). This should not be surprising given that the anomie from being a "lesser citizen" unworthy of shelter during a life threatening storm may make some former offenders turn to mechanisms for survival that return them to prison.

Further, many offenders recidivate due to the expensive negative impacts of fines and court costs that result in warrants and negatively impacts well-being (Whittle 2018).

These collateral consequences do not generally differentiate between a murderer and a three-strike felon convicted of two drug possessions and a shoplifting charge. Moreover, the things that constitute a felony charge have expanded in the "Get Tough" era of mass incarceration. These policies have been linked to recidivism due to the limitations they pose on re-entry once they adhere to an individual (Mele and Miller 2005; Saxonhouse 2004). This has led to many activists to call for a desistance-based probation system and toward ending collateral consequences in general (Ewald and Rottinghaus 2009; Uggen and Inderbitzin 2009; Farrall 2004).

Life with a Warrant in a Time of Natural Disaster

There are approximately two million individuals in the United States with an active warrant and half of all arrests are derived from warrants (Bierie 2014). There is a lacuna in criminal justice research on warrants. When people hear the term *fugitive* or *warrant*, it may suggest the idea of a "murderer on the run" (Goldkamp and Vîlcică 2008; Bierie 2014). The reality is that most individuals with a warrant are lacking in social capital and skills rather than being dangerous fugitives (Goldkamp and White 2006). In fact, individuals with a warrant are a tempting target for predators because they cannot utilize the civil resources available (Goffman 2009).

Goffman highlights this phenomenon by recounting the story of "Alex," who went with his girlfriend to the hospital deliver their child. While there on an unrelated assault call, police checked the visitor log and found that he had a warrant for a drinking violation to his parole. "Alex" was arrested in the delivery room and spent a year in custody, leading other men to avoid going with their partners to deliver children (Goffman 2009). It is possible to extrapolate from this to anticipate what may happen in future natural disasters: If it is understood that taking care of one's physical safety may result in more time behind bars, fewer people will be willing to do so (especially since many in the community may be unsure if they have a warrant or not). An illustration of even greater concern is that of Nicholas Bowen: he was arrested four times, was sent to Rikers Island three times, and was even shackled to a hospital bed . . . all for a warrant that never should have been issued in the first place (Feuer 2016).

Warrants are issued for a vast variety of charges. Most are issued for court offenses such as failure to appear, failing to obey a court order, or violating community corrections. Two counties actually found that half of all warrants were court violations and 75 percent of those were actually traffic offenses.

By way of illustration, Goffman looked at a specific area in Philadelphia (one of social disorganization where offenders are likely to return to) and found that of 308 men between 18 and 30, 144 had a warrant for court fines or failure to appear and another 119 had warrants for technical violations to their probation or parole (Goffman 2009). When most people think of those with multiple traffic violations, they likely don't consider not being able to utilize disaster response as an appropriate collateral consequence.

More prisoners are released conditionally than ever before, meaning they have conditions that must be adhered to or risk returning to prison (Visher and Travis 2003). The surveillance-focused probation and parole system leads to a life for many formerly incarcerated individuals (as well as those involved with community corrections) that is marked by fear returning back to prison. It should be noted that the most marginalized group, sex offenders, are even less likely to abscond than other offender groups (Williams et al. 2000).

SEX OFFENDER STATUS IN AMERICA

The most severe collateral consequences are reserved for sex offenders and in general the public supports these harsher punitive collateral consequences (Rogers et al. 2011; Viki et al. 2012; Bollinger et al. 2012). SORNA restrictions have not been found to have an impact on recidivism (Duwe and Donnay 2008; Madden et al. 2011; Tewksbury and Jennings 2010). Sex offender registries and the public notifications of sexual offenders began in 1994 with the Jacob Wetterling Act of 1994. In 1996, Megan's Law was passed that required all states to have registries with community notification. A decade later, Florida's Jessica's Law (2005) mandated increased surveillance of offenders (although this failed to pass federally) and the Adam Walsh Act (also referred to as the Sex Offender Registration and Notification Act - SORNA) in 2006 set minimum guidelines for sex offenders regardless of the state they live in (Tabachnick and McCartan 2017). The resulting requirements vary by state, but all involve public notification of sexual offenders and exclusion zones that limit where sex offenders can live (e.g., away from schools, parks, daycares, bus stops or other places children congregate).

Sex offender registries are based largely on sensationalized media accounts of children that mediated the risk for the public and for legislators (Sample and Kadleck 2008; Petrunik 2003; Tabachnick and McCartan 2017). The unfortunate side effect of this is a skewed focus on adults who assault children outside of their family. This leads to policy that does not reflect the truth about sexual victimization and that leaves individuals with the idea that sex offenders are a constant threat to strangers and that isolation is the only solution to protect the public good (Hanvey et al. 2011; McCartan 2010, 2013)

Although parents are more likely to warn their children about "stranger danger" and people who view the registries are also more likely to be concerned with victimization by strangers, the reality is that most sexual offenders abuse someone close to them (Collins 1996; Wurtele et al. 1992; Craun and Theriot 2009). Further, there is a perception that sex offenders almost always recidivate, when in reality sex offenders are rearrested less frequently than non-sex offenders and most sexual offenders will not commit another crime (Greenfield 1997; Hanson and Bussiere 1998; Quinsey et al. 1995). Even when faced with the reality of this low percentage, we find that people believe there is a high likelihood of reoffense. For example, Knighton and his colleagues asked jurors if they considered a 1 percent chance to be "likely to reoffend." Over 53.6 percent said "yes," while 82.7 percent of jurors agreed that someone with at 15 percent chance of recidivism was "likely to reoffend" (Knighton et al. 2014).

Sex offender registries have been repeatedly found to have little impact on recidivism of sex offenses (Socia and Stamatel 2010; Lasher and McGrath 2012; Levenson and Cotter 2005). Further, the laws tend to be a more symbolic means to reassure the public that something is being done (even if it is based on the myth of the stranger attacker). However, law enforcement and policymakers still support these mandates (regardless of the data that they do not reduce recidivism) even while admitting the negative consequences they can pose for offenders reentry (Meloy et al. 2013; Walfield et al. 2017; Mustaine et al. 2015). It is important to note that although the protective impacts are not realized, the negative impacts on offender reintegration are very real, including the likelihood that the offender moves to a socially disorganized neighborhood or picks up an additional felony for housing restriction violations or failure to report (Levenson et al. 2015; Jeglic et al. 2011).

The Family of Sex Offenders

While the benefits of registries have mixed results at best, there is no doubt that sex offender registries have large-scale impacts on both offenders and their families, particularly in the realms of housing and employment (Whittle 2018). Sex offenders report having difficulty obtaining housing and jobs and a majority experience negative psychological consequences. Sexual offenders report that they have experienced harassment by neighbors (44 percent), having their property damaged (14 percent), job loss (30 percent), and housing disruptions and instability (31 percent) (Lasher and McGrath 2012).

It is important to note, that it is not just the offenders themselves, but also their families that experience this. The families of sex offenders experience a host of negative aspects (Farkas and Miller 2007; Levenson and Cotter 2005). In 2009 Levenson and Tweksbury conducted a survey of the families of sexual offenders, in which they found that 82 percent experienced financial hardship, 44 percent were harassed, and 7 percent were physically assaulted. Of the 95 children involved in the survey, 80 percent experienced anger, 77 percent experienced depression and 65 percent felt left out from their peers in school and activities (Levenson and Tewksbury 2009). The compounding of these factors and experiences during a natural disaster are immeasurable. In general, families tend to make collective decisions when deciding whether to seek shelter care during a natural disaster. As such, it is reasonable to assume that if the offender is not welcome, the family will also not be able to access safety.

Sex Offenders with Intellectual Disabilities and Disaster Preparation

By definition, natural disasters are profoundly dangerous and disruptive to all who experience them. However, danger and disruption profoundly increase with regard to people with intellectual disabilities, who are at especially high risk during disasters, as noted by Stough (2015), "People with intellectual disabilities, regardless of the type of environmental hazard they encounter, are more likely to need additional assistance during evacuation, experience more tangible losses during disaster, and need additional support in the recovery phase following disaster" (p. 142). The intersection of natural disaster, intellectual disability, and a third component, status as a sex offender, create an exceedingly vulnerable population with regard to disaster preparedness.

Historically collateral consequences of incarceration including sex offenders were referred to as "civil disabilities," and we have discussed how these disabilities extend to the civil aspects of disaster preparedness (most notably shelter care). There is a group of people who are at risk of experiencing a double jeopardy as it relates to unequal treatment described to this point: those with intellectual disabilities (ID) who have criminal records, including sex offenses (and are thus doubly discriminated against with civil disabilities as well). The fifth edition of the *American Psychiatric Association's Diagnostic and Statistical Manual* defines ID as:

- Deficits in intellectual functioning, including reasoning; problem solving; planning; abstract thinking; judgment; academic learning; and experiential learning
- Deficits or impairments in adaptive functioning including communication; social skills; personal independence in home or community settings; and school or work functioning
- These limitations occur before the age of 21 (American Psychiatric Association 2013)

People with ID make up approximately 2–3 percent of the general population but are estimated to comprise 2–10 percent of the population of people in prison or jail (Fogden et al. 2016; Fazel et al. 2008; Petersilia 2000). The Arc, a leading advocacy organization for people with ID, notes that people with ID are at increased risk for violations of the law and incarceration:

> Almost all people with intellectual disabilities now live in the community and are susceptible to becoming involved in the criminal justice system as suspects and/or victims. As suspects, individuals with this disability are frequently used by other criminals to assist in law-breaking activities without understanding their involvement in a crime or the consequences of their involvement. This may also have a strong need to be accepted and may agree to help with criminal activities in order to gain friendship. (Davis 2013)

The attributes and vulnerabilities that are present for people with ID relative to the criminal justice system are amplified when it comes to sex-related offenses. People with ID are at significantly higher risk than the general population for both victimization by sexual offenders and for committing sexual offenses (Fogden et al. 2016; Davis 2013; Petersilia 2000). Because stigmatized social constructions of people with ID abound, one of the consequences of communities not understanding people with ID as capable of the full spectrum of human experiences may be the denial of sex and sexuality as part of the identity of people with ID. Functionally, this may translate into a profound lack of sex-related educational opportunities and resources for this population.

As a consequence, people with ID may lack socialization around and opportunities for sexual expression and behavior. Therefore, when these behaviors occur in a way that violate broader social norms and the behaviors are sanctioned, the person with ID is further marginalized. Thus, problematic behaviors that may be expressed by someone with ID (e.g., public urination, self-stimulation/masturbation, etc.) should be interpreted much differently than the same behavior evidenced by a member of the general population, but this is often not the case. This is especially challenging when it comes to people with mild ID, who may not have this disability identified by community supports. Petersilia (2000, p. 10) noted that "the Department of Justice reports that most prison inmates with retardation fall within the mild [ID] category, although some are within the moderate [ID] range . . . If the social service system hasn't officially identified people as having [ID] or developmental disabilities, and police are untrained and often fail to recognize people with [ID], then it is no wonder that people with developmental disabilities move through arrest, conviction, incarceration without anyone taking notice."

The link between having an intellectual disability and being at-risk for sexual acting-out (which may include commission of sexual offences) is significant. Fogden et al. (2016) report that they found rates of sexual offending by people with ID occurred at rates 18 times greater than that of the general population, while more conservative estimates still identify significantly higher rates of offences (Fazel et al. 2008; Davis 2013; Lambrick and Glaser 2004; Lindsay 2002). In many cases, people with ID may lack of information or understanding about sex, sexuality, and sexual behavior. Deficits in adaptive functioning and social skills related to relationships, touch, communication, and consent may compound this, as do difficulties in self-regulation of emotions as well as impaired impulse control. These factors and others combine to create higher risk for people with ID for becoming victims of sexual abuse and assault, higher risk for committing sexual offences, and for heightened vulnerability to natural disasters.

Deficits in cognition and adaptive behavior experienced by people with ID not only create risks for victimization by and perpetration of sexual offences, but also create a high degree of risk in natural disasters and other large-scale disruptions of supportive services. Priestly and Hemingway (2006, p. 29) note that disruptions and damage to infrastructure represent significant difficulties to everyone, "disabled people may be disproportionately disadvantaged by depletion of both physical infrastructure and human services." Therefore, in the social and physical disruptions that occur in a natural disaster, offenders with ID are at extreme vulnerability with regard to accessing (or being permitted to access) emergency shelters and services, as well as being left out of recovery and development efforts that occur in the wake of a disaster. These three dimensions (i.e., intellectual disability, labeling as a sex offender, and disruption of services as a result of natural disaster) need to be accounted for in disaster preparation, response, and rebuilding, including access to shelter care.

THE CASE OF FLORIDA

Florida offers a unique look at the impact of collateral consequences of SORNA and other forms of criminal justice impact on individuals experiencing a natural disaster. Chiricos and colleagues found that people formally labeled as felon in Florida had higher likelihood to recidivate within two years than similar law breakers that voided the felon label (Chiricos et al. 2007). Florida has some of the more stringent sex offender registry limitations in the country and have well documented problems with sex offenders being able to find appropriate housing once they are on the registry. Further, Florida has the highest percentage of the African American electorate lacking the ability to vote due to felon disenfranchisement, with 23 percent of this community unable to vote (Uggen and Manza 2004). It has been estimated that if less than 1 percent of adult male felons in Florida would have voted in the 2000 election, it would have tipped the scales in Al Gore's favor (Preuhs 2001; Uggen and Manza 2004).

When it comes to warrants, Bierie found that Florida had the most active warrants of any state in the United States with 309,032 (15.81 percent of all warrants); they were fourth in the nation per capita (Bierie 2014). Further, Flannery and Kretchsmar (2012) reported on the safe surrender program where people could come to a site to see if they had a warrant and then turn themselves in. One of the sites was located in Florida. The Florida site saw fewer surrenders than any other site by far, with only 163 individuals (by comparison, the highest was in Cleveland, OH with 7431). Additionally, the Florida site saw that a higher percentage of those individuals who submitted did not actually have a warrant (24.5 percent in Florida compared to 18 percent overall). Of those that did have a warrant, 12.2 percent were arrested as compared to the average of around 2 percent (Flannery and Kretschmar 2012). This further reinforcing the perception that law enforcement in Florida is harsher than elsewhere in the United States. Over 60 percent of those utilizing the safe surrender program heard about it through the media. Meaning they are also likely to hear through the media that they will be arrested or, in the case of a disaster, turned away from a shelter.

In Florida's Polk County specifically, Sheriff Grady Judd has been with the Sheriff's office since 1972. He was elected sheriff in 2004 and has been re-elected three times. He has proven to be a controversial public figure, with numerous racial profiling complaints and claims of police overreach, including the shooting of African American Angilo Freeland who was shot 68 times during a standoff. When asked why Freeland was shot that many times, the sheriff replied, "That's all the bullets we had" (Associated Press 2006). Judd preaches in churches in his uniform and has removed basketball hoops from his jails to donate to churches (Palm 2010). He also seems to prefer stigma and shaming as methods of policing, publicizing stings of prostitutes and johns in March as "March Sadness" (Para 2017). In short, Sheriff Judd was no stranger to controversy when his #Irma tweets went out.

Individuals placed on Florida's sex offender registry remain on the registry until one year after their death. Non-aggravated indecent exposure and public urination as well as statutory rape (if the victim is over sixteen and the perpetrator is under twenty-four years of age) are not registerable crimes. Registrants are required to give twice yearly updates for offenders and four times yearly updates for those adjudicated as predators, and they must update within 48 hours of any change in residence even if temporary (such as going to a shelter). Failure to comply with any aspect of the registry is a felony. Florida also has a sexual predator secondary adjudication for those deemed likely to reoffend, and, under the *Jimmy Ryce Sexually Violent Predator Act,* Florida has the ability to civilly commit sex offenders after their criminal sentences are served if they are deemed dangerous sexual predators. This effectively removes the most dangerous sexual offenders from concern during natural disasters and limits the protective claim of Sheriff Judd's tweets.

On September 7, 2017, when the tweets went public, we memorialized all of the current offender registrants in Polk County (1,171 sex offenders at the time). This allowed us to present a snapshot of who the residents were who endured the collateral consequences of not having a shelter during the hurricane. We found the age of the offenders during the hurricane ranged from 14 to 91 with an average age of 50.07 (SD 13.75). The average age at which their first registerable crime ranged from 14 to 84 with an average of 34.13 (SD 12.07). The years since they last committed a sex crime ranged from 0 to 56 years with an average time since any sexual offense being 15.06 years (standard deviation 8.01). Over 9.1 percent of the offenders were adjudicated as predators. Over 80.7 percent of registrants were identified as White and the remaining 19.2 percent were identified as Black (the Florida registry does not provide an indicator for Hispanic ancestry). The vast majority were males (97.3 percent) and most had been completely released for corrections (70.5 percent) with only 28.5 percent still under supervision. Only 5.2 percent of the offenders had committed a second offense after their first registered sex crime.

Florida Epilogue

In 2007, then-Governor Charlie Christ amended the process for executive clemency and allowed more felons to be reenfranchised, doing so after winning an election in a landslide victory (Phillips and Deckard 2016). However four years later, when Rick Scott became the governor after a tight race, the enfranchisement process tightened sharply again. Finally, during the contentious 2018 election, the people of Florida themselves voted to reenfranchise felons in the state. This likely stems from having gone too far with collateral consequences, as highlighted by Sheriff Grady Judd's Tweets during Hurricane Irma. While this may change the electorate in Florida, more importantly it may allow offenders to have a more active stake in civil society and expand social capital. The same people who were singled out by Sheriff Judd for unequal civil protections will now be able to participate in civil society, including weighing in on his fitness for the office.

CONCLUSION

In summary, the actions of Sheriff Judd in Florida can be understood as an extension of the so-called collateral consequences of incarceration, particularly in relation to sex offenders. After serving their time, offenders find complete reintegration to be unavailable and, worse still, the most serious barriers show up in the most crucial times in their lives (as illustrated by the Twitter reminder that they cannot seek public shelter during a hurricane). The impacts of these policies are not confined to the offenders themselves, with the spillover reaching their families and ultimately the community as a whole. It is additionally compounded for those who have intellectual disabilities that are already disadvantaged by their disability status and doubly so with the stigma of a record. Many of the policies of collateral consequence exclusion are being remedied through legislation and social activism, drawing attention to the issue of disaster response that will hopefully add this dimension to the collateral consequences that should be erased for offenders, allowing a complete re-entry into society for the benefit of all.

NOTE

1. Corresponding author. A version of this paper was presented at the 2018 North Central Sociological Association.

REFERENCES

American Psychiatric Association. 2013. *Diagnostic and Statistical Manual of Mental Disorders.* 5th ed. Arlington, VA: American Psychiatric Publishing.

Associated Press. 2006. "Florida Police Shot Suspected Cop Killer 68 Times." *Fox News,* June 2006. https://www.foxnews.com/story/florida-police-shot-suspected-cop-killer-68-times.

Bahr, Stephen J., Anita Harker Armstrong, Benjamin Guild Gibbs, Paul E. Harris, and James K. Fisher. 2005. "The Reentry Process: How Parolees Adjust to Release from Prison." *Fathering: Harriman* 3 (3): 243. http://dx.doi.org/10.3149/fth.0303.243.

Behrens, Angela, Christopher Uggen, and Jeff Manza. 2003. "Ballot Manipulation and the 'Menace of Negro Domination': Racial Threat and Felon Disenfranchisement in the United States, 1850–2002." *American Journal of Sociology* 109: 559–605.

Bierie, David M. 2014. "Fugitives in the United States." *Journal of Criminal Justice* 42 (4): 327–37. https://doi.org/10.1016/j.jcrimjus.2014.04.005.

Blumstein, Alfred, and Allen J. Beck. 1999. "Population Growth in U.S. Prisons, 1980–1996." *Crime and Justice* 26: 17–61.

Bollinger, Jenna, Katie Seidler, and Richard Kemp. 2012. "Who Thinks What About Child Protection: Community Perceptions and Awareness of Child Protection

Strategies and Their Effectiveness for Reducing Sexual Offending." *Sexual Abuse in Australia and New Zealand* 4 (1): 33–40.

Bradley, Katherine H., and R. B. Michael Oliver. 2001. *No Place Like Home: Housing and the Ex-Prisoner Policy Brief.* Boston, MA: Community Resources for Justice.

Bruce, Matt, Sarah Crowley, Nikki Jeffcote, and Belinda Coulston. 2014. "Community DSPD Pilot Services in South London: Rates of Reconviction and Impact of Supported Housing on Reducing." *Criminal Behavior and Mental Health* 24: 129–40.

Carlson, P. M. 2004. "Something to Lose: A Balanced and Reality-Based Rational for Institutional Programming." In *Crime and Employment: Critical Issues in Crime Reduction for Corrections*, edited by Jessie L. Krienert and Mark S. Fleisher, 61–74. Walnut Creek, CA: AltaMira Press.

Chiricos, Ted, Kelle Barrick, William Bales, and Stephanie Bontrager. 2007. "The Labeling of Convicted Felons and Its Consequences for Recidivism." *Criminology* 45: 547–81.

Clark, Lynn M. 2007. "Landlord Attitudes Toward Renting to Released Offenders*." *Federal Probation* 71 (1): 20–30, 60. Washington.

Clear, Todd. 2007. *Imprisoning Communities: How Mass Incarceration Makes Disadvantaged Neighborhoods Worse.* New York: Oxford University Press.

Clear, Todd R., Diana R. Rose, and Judith A. Ryder. 2001. "Incarceration and the Community: The Problem of Removing and Returning Offenders." *Crime and Delinquency* 47 (3): 335–51.

Coleman, James. 1988. "Social Capital in the Creation of Human Capital." *American Journal of Sociology* 94: s95–120.

Collins, Mary Elizabeth. 1996. "Parents' Perceptions of the Risk of Child Sexual Abuse and Their Protective Behaviors: Findings from a Qualitative Study." *Child Maltreatment* 1: 53–64.

Craun, Sarah W., and Matthew T. Theriot. 2009. "Misperceptions of Sex Offender Perpetration: Considering the Impact of Sex Offender Registration." *Journal of Interpersonal Violence* 24 (12): 2057–72. https://doi.org/10.1177/0886260508327706.

Curtin, Elizabeth. 2005. "Home Sweet Home for Ex-Offenders." In *Civil Penalties, Social Consequences*, edited by Christopher Mele and Teresa A. Miller, 111–20. United Kingdom: Routledge.

Davis, Leigh Ann. 2013. *People with Intellectual Disabilities in the Criminal Justice Systems: Victims & Suspects.* Washington, DC: The Arc of the United States. http://thearc.org/wp-content/uploads/2019/07/Criminal%20Justice%20System.pdf.

Duwe, Grant, and William Donnay. 2008. "The Impact of Megan's Law on Sex Offender Recidvism: The Minnesota Experience." *Criminology* 46: 411–46.

Ewald, Alec C., and Brandon Rottinghaus. 2009. *Criminal Disenfranchisement in an International Perspective.* New York: Cambridge University Press.

Farkas, Mary Ann, and Gale Miller. 2007. "Reentry and Reintegration: Challenges Faced by Families of Convicted Sex Offenders." *Federal Sentencing Reporter* 20: 88–92.

Farrall, Stephen. 2004. "Social Capital and Offender Reintegration: Making Probation Desistance Focused." In *After Crime and Punishment: Pathways to Offender Reintegration*, edited by Shadd Maruna and Russ Immarigeon. Portland, OR: Willan Publishing.

Fazel, Seena, Kiriakos Xeenitidis, and John Powell. 2008. "The Prevalence of Intellectual Disabiltites Among 12000 Prisoners: A Systematic Review." *International Journal of Law and Psychiatry* 31 (4): 369–73.

Feuer, Alan. 2016. "Cleared of a Crime but Hounded by a Warrant." *The New York Times* (New York, NY), March 29, 2016. https://www.nytimes.com/2016/03/29/nyregion/cleared-of-a-crime-but-hounded-by-a-warrant.html.

Flannery, Daniel J., and Jeff M. Kretschmar. 2012. "Fugitive Safe Surrender." *Criminology & Public Policy* 11 (3): 437–59. https://doi.org/10.1111/j.1745-9133.2012.00821.x.

Fogden, Billy C., Stuart D. M. Thomas, Michael Daffern, and James R. P. Ogloff. 2016. "Crime and Victimisation in People with Intellectual Disability: A Case Linkage Study." *BMC Psychiatry* 16 (1): 170. https://doi.org/10.1186/s12888-016-0869-7.

Goffman, Alice. 2009. "On the Run: Wanted Men in a Philadelphia Ghetto." *American Sociological Review* 74 (3): 339–57.

Goldkamp, John S., and E. Rely Vîlcică. 2008. "Targeted Enforcement and Adverse System Side Effects: The Generation of Fugitives in Philadelphia*." *Criminology* 46 (2): 371–409. https://doi.org/10.1111/j.1745-9125.2008.00113.x.

Goldkamp, John S., and Michael D. White. 2006. "Restoring Accountability in Pretrial Release: The Philadelphia Pretrial Release Supervision Experiments." *Journal of Experimental Criminology* 2: 143–81.

Greenfield, Lawrence. 1997. *Sex Offenses and Offenders: An Analysis of Data on Rape and Sexual Assault*. Washington DC: U.S. Department of Justice, Bureau of Justice Statistics, Office of Justice Programs.

Handelsman, Lauren. 2005. "Giving the Barking Dog a Bite: Challenging Felon Disenfranchisement under the Voting Rights Act of 1965." *Fordham Law Review* 73: 1875–940.

Hanson, Karl B., and Monique T. Bussiere. 1998. "Predicting Relapse: A Meta-Analysis of Sexual Offender Recidivism Studies." *Journal of Consulting and Clinical Psychology* 66: 348–62.

Hanvey, Stephen, Terry Philpot, and Chris WIlson. 2011. *A Community-Based Approach to the Reduction of Sexual Reoffending*. London: Jessica Kinglsey Publishers.

Harding, David J., Jessica J. B. Wyse, Cheyney Dobson, and Jeffrey D. Morenoff. 2014. "Making Ends Meet After Prison." *Journal of Policy Analysis and Management* 33: 440–70.

Helfgott, Jacqueline. 1997. "Ex-Offender Needs Versus Community Opportunity in Seattle." *Federal Probation* 61 (2): 12.

Hill, Kim Q. 1994. *Democracy in the Fifth States*. Lincoln, NE: University of Nebraska Press.

Hirschi, Travis. 1969. *Causes of Delinquency*. Berkeley: University of California Press.

Jeglic, Elizabeth, Cynthia Calkins Mercado, and Jill S. Levenson. 2011. "The Prevalence and Correlates of Depression and Hopelessness among Sex Offenders Subject to Community Notification and Residence Restriction Legislation." *Journal of Criminal Justice* 37 (1): 46–59.

Knighton, Jefferson C., Daniel C. Murrie, Marcus T. Boccaccini, and Darrel B. Turner. 2014. "How Likely Is 'Likely to Reoffend' in Sex Offender Civil Commitment Trials?" *Law and Human Behavior* 38 (3): 293–304. http://dx.doi.org/10.1037/lhb0000079.

LaFollette, Hugh. 2005. "Collateral Consequences of Punishment: Civil Penalties Accompanying Formal Punishment." *Journal of Applied Philosophy* 22: 241–61.

Lambrick, Frank, and William Glaser. 2004. "Sex Offenders with Intellectual Disability." *Sexual Abuse* 16 (4): 381–92.

Lasher, Michael P., and Robert J. McGrath. 2012. "The Impact of Community Notification on Sex Offender Reintegration: A Quantitative Review of the Research Literature." *International Journal of Offender Therapy and Comparative Criminology* 56 (1): 6–28. https://doi.org/10.1177/0306624X10387524.

Laub, John H., and Robert J. Sampson. 2001. "Understanding Desistance from Crime." *Crime and Justice* 28: 1–69.

Levenson, Jill, Alissa Ackerman, Kelly M. Socia, and Andrew J. Harris. 2015. "Where for Art Thou? Transient Sex Offenders and Residence Restrictions." *Criminal Justice Policy Review* 26 (4): 319–44.

Levenson, Jill, and Richard Tewksbury. 2009. "Collateral Damage: Family Members of Registered Sex Offenders." *American Journal of Criminal Justice* 34 (1): 54–68. https://doi.org/10.1007/s12103-008-9055-x.

Levenson, Jill S., and Leo P. Cotter. 2005. "The Effect of Megan's Law on Sex Offender Reintegration." *International Journal of Criminal Justice* 21: 49–66.

Lindsay, W. R. 2002. "Research and Literature on Sex Offenders with Intellectual and Developmental Disability Research." *Journal of Intellectual Disability Research* 46 (1S): 74–85.

Lynch, James P., William J. Sabol, Michael Planty, and Mary Shelly. n.d. "Crime, Coercion and Community: The Effects of Arrest and Incarceration Policies on Informal Social Control in Neighborhoods, Executive Summary." 20.

Madden, Sean, J. M. Miller, Jeffrey T. Walker, and Inekettarn H. Marshall. 2011. "Utilizing Criminal History Information to Explore the Effect of Community Notification on Sex Offender Recidivism." *Justice Quarterly* 28: 303–24.

Mauer, Meda, and Marc Chesney-Lind. 2002. *Invisible Punishment: The Collateral Consequences of Mass Imprisonment.* New York, NY: The New Press.

McCartan, Kieran F. 2010. "Student/Trainee-Professional Implicit Theories of Paedophilia." *Psychology, Crime and Law* 16: 265–88.

———. 2013. "From a Lack of Engagement and Mistrust to Partnership? Public Attitudes to the Disclosure of Sex Offender Information." *International Journal of Police Science and Management* 13: 219–36.

Mele, Christopher, and Teresa A. Miller. 2005. "Collateral Civil Penalties as Techniques of Social Policy." In *Civil Penalties, Social Consequences*, edited by Christopher Mele and Teresa A. Miller. New York and London: Routledge.

Meloy, Michelle, Kristin Curtis, and Jessica Boatwright. 2013. "The Sponsors of Sex Offender Bills Speak Up: Policy Makers' Perceptions of Sex Offenders, Sex Crimes, and Sex Offender Legislation." *Criminal Justice and Behavior* 40 (4): 438–52. https://doi.org/10.1177/0093854812455740.

Metraux, S., and D. P. Culhane. 2004. "Homeless Shelter Use and Reincarceration Following Prison Release." *Criminology & Public Policy* 3: 139–60.

Miller, Bryan Lee, and Joseph F. Spillane. 2012. "Civil Death: An Examination of Ex-Felon Disenfranchisement and Reintegration." *Punishment & Society* 14 (4): 402–28. https://doi.org/10.1177/1462474512452513.

Mustaine, Elizabeth E., Richard Tewksbury, David P. Connor, and Brian K. Payne. 2015. "Criminal Justice Officials' Views of Sex Offenders, Sex Offender Registration, Community Notification, and Residency Restrictions." *Justice System Journal* 36 (1): 63–85.

Pager, Devah. 2007. *Marked: Race, Crime, and Finding Work in an Era of Mass Incarceration.* Chicago, IL: University of Chicago Press.

Palm, Anika Myers. 2010. "Polk Sheriff Removes Basketball from Jail, Donates Equipment to Churches." *Orlando Sentinel*, December 23, 2010.

Para, Eric. 2017. "Polk County Sheriff's Office: Operation March Sadness Nets 104 Suspects." *The Ledger*, March 21, 2017.

Petersilia, Joan. 2000. *Doing Justice? Criminal Offenders with Developmental Disabilities. Detailed Research Findings.* Berkeley, CA: California Policy Research Center. https://www.ncjrs.gov/App/Publications/abstract.aspx?ID=185053.

Petrunik, Michael. 2003. "The Hare and the Tortoise: Dangerousness and Sex Offender Policy in the United States and Canada." *Canadian Journal of Criminology and Criminal Justice* 45: 43–72.

Phillips, Anthony Jamal, and Natalie Deckard. 2016. "Felon Disenfranchisement Laws and the Feedback Loop of Political Exclusion: The Case of Florida." *Journal of African American Studies* 20 (1): 1–18. https://doi.org/10.1007/s12111 -015-9314-0.

Pinard, Michael. 2009. "Collateral Consequences of Criminal Convictions: Confronting Issues of Race and Dignity." *New York University Law Review* 85: 457.

Preuhs, Robert R. 2001. "State Felon Disenfranchisement Policy." *Social Science Quarterly* 82 (4): 733–48. https://doi.org/10.1111/0038-4941.00056.

Priestly, Mark, and Laura Hemingway. 2008. "Disability and Disaster Recovery." *Journal of Social Work in Disability & Rehabilitation* 5 (3–4): 23–42.

Quinsey, Vernon, Marnie Rice, and Grant Harris. 1995. "Actuarial Prediction of Sexual Recidivism." *Journal of Interpersonal Violence* 10 (1): 85–105.

Roberts, Dorothy D. 2004. "The Social and Moral Cost of Mass Incarceration in African American Communities." *Stanford Law Review* 56: 1271–305.

Rogers, Paul, Lindsay Hirst, and Michelle Davies. 2011. "An Investigation into the Effect of Respondent Gender, Victim Age, and Perpetrator Treatment on Public Attitudes Towards Sex Offenders, Sex Offender Treatment, and Sex Offender Rehabilitation." *Journal of Offender Rehabilitation* 50 (8): 511–30.

Roman, Catrina Gouvis. 2004. "A Roof Is Not Enough: Successful Prisoner Reintegration Requires Experimentation and Collaboration." *Criminology and Public Policy* 3 (2): 161–68.

Sample, Lisa L., and Colleen Kadleck. 2008. "Sex Offender Laws: Legislators' Accounts of the Need for Policy." *Criminal Justice Policy Review* 19: 40–62.

Sampson, Robert J. 2002. "The Community." In *Crime Public Policies for Crime Control*, edited by James Q. Wilson and Joan Petersilia, 225–52. Oakland, CA: ICS Press.

Sampson, Robert J., and John H. Laub. 1993. *Crime in the Making: Pathways and Turning Points Through Life*. Cambridge, MA: Harvard University Press.

Sampson, Robert J., Stephen W. Raudenbush, and Felton Earls. 1997. "Neighborhoods and Violent Crime: A Multilevel Study of Collective Efficacy." *Science* 277 (5328): 918–24. https://doi.org/10.1126/science.277.5328.918.

Saxonhouse, Elena. 2004. "Unequal Protection: Comparing Former Felons' Challenges to Disenfranchisement and Employment Discrimination." *Stanford Law Review* 56 (6): 1597–639.

Shanahan, Colleen. 2012. "Significant Entanglements: A Framework for the Civil Consequences of Criminal Convictions." *American Criminal Law Review* 49: 1387–436.

Shapiro, Andrew L. 1993. "Challenging Criminal Disenfranchisement Under the Voting Rights Act: A New Strategy." *The Yale Law Journal* 103 (2): 537. https://doi.org/10.2307/797104.

Socia, Kelly M., and Janet P. Stamatel. 2010. "Assumptions and Evidence Behind Sex Offender Laws: Registration, Community Notification and Residence Restrictions." *Sociology Compass* 4: 1–20.

Sohoni, Tracy W. P. 2014. *The Effects of Collateral Consequence Laws on State Rates of Returns to Prison*. Doctoral Dissertation. MD: University of Maryland.

Solomon, Amy L., Caterina Gouvis, and Michelle Waul. 2001. "Summary of Focus Group with Ex-Prisoners in the District: Ingredients for Successful Reintegration: (717962011-001)." *American Psychological Association*. https://doi.org/10.1037/e717962011-001.

Stough, Laura M. 2015. "World Report on Disability, Intellectual Disabilities, and Disaster Preparedness: Costa Rica as a Case Example." *Journal of Policy and Practice in Intellectual Disabilities* 12 (2): 138–46.

Tabachnick, Joan, and Kieran McCartan. 2017. "Sexual Harm, Public Education and Risk Management." In *Contemporary Sex Offender Risk Management, Volume I: Perceptions*, edited by Kieran McCartan and Hazel Kemshall, 61–87. Palgrave Studies in *Risk, Crime and Society*. Cham: Springer International Publishing. https://doi.org/10.1007/978-3-319-63567-5_3.

Taylor, Caitlin J. 2013. "The Supervision to Aid Reentry (STAR) Programme: Enhancing the Social Capital of Ex-Offenders." *Probation Journal* 60 (2): 119–35. https://doi.org/10.1177/0264550513478319.

Tewksbury, Richard, and Wesley G. Jennings. 2010. "Assessing the Impact of Sex Offender Registration and Community Notification on Sex-Offending Trajectories." *Criminal Justice and Behavior* 37: 507–82.

Travis, Jeremy, Amy L. Solomon, and Michelle Waul. 2001. "From Prison to Home: The Dimensions and Consequences of Prisoner Reentry: (720982011-001)." *American Psychological Association*. https://doi.org/10.1037/e720982011-001.

Travis, Jeremy, and Sarah Lawrence. 2002. *Beyond the Gate: The State of Parole in America*. Washington, DC: The Urban Institute.

Uggen, Christopher, and Jeff Manza. 2004. "Punishment and Democracy: Disenfranchisement of Nonincarcerated Felons in the United States." *Perspectives on Politics* 2 (3): 491–505.

Uggen, Christopher, Jeff Manza, and Melissa Thompson. 2003. "Citizenship, Democracy, and the Civic Reintegration of Criminal Offenders." *The Annals of the American Academy of Political and Social Science* 605: 281–310.

Uggen, Christopher, and Michelle Inderbitzin. 2009. "The Price and the Promise of Citizenship: Extending the Vote to Non-Incarcerated Felons." *American Society of Criminology Policy Essay*. http://www.soc.umn.edu/~uggen/uggen_inderbitzen_asc_09.pdf.

Viki, G., Iona Fullerton, Hannah Raggett, Fiona Tait, and Suzanne Wiltshire. 2012. "The Role of Dehumanization in Attitudes Toward the Social Exclusion and Rehabilitation of Sex Offenders." *Journal of Applied Social Psychology* 42 (10): 2349–67.

Visher, Christy, Demelza Baer, and Rebecca Naser. 2006. *Ohio Prisoners' Reflections on Returning Home*. Washington, DC: The Urban Institute.

Visher, Christy A., and Jeremy Travis. 2003. "Transitions from Prison to Community: Understanding Individual Pathways." *Annual Review of Sociology* 29 (1): 89–113. https://doi.org/10.1146/annurev.soc.29.010202.095931.

Walfield, Scott M., Jill S. Levenson, Michelle A. Cubellis, Andrew J. Harris, and Christopher Lobanov-Rostovsky. 2017. "Law Enforcement Views on Sex Offender Compliance with Registration Mandates." *American Journal of Criminal Justice* 42 (4): 807–32. https://doi.org/10.1007/s12103-017-9386-6.

Western, Bruce. 2007. *Punishment and Inequality in America*. New York: Russell Sage Foundation.

Whittle, Tanya N. 2018. "Felony Collateral Sanctions Effects on Recidivism: A Literature Review." *Criminal Justice Policy Review* 29 (5): 505–24. https://doi.org/10.1177/0887403415623328.

Williams, Frank P., Marilyn D. McShane, and H. Michael Dolny. 2000. "Predicting Parole Absconders." *Prison Journal* 80 (1): 24–38.

Wurtele, Sandy K., Mary Kvaternick, and Corrina F. Franklin. 1992. "Sexual Abuse Prevention for Preschoolers: A Survey of Parents' Behaviors, Attitudes and Beliefs." *Journal of Child Sexual Abuse* 1: 113–28.

Wynn, Jennifer R. 2012. "Inside Rikers: The Social Impact of Mass Incarceration in the Twenty-First Century." *Judges' Journal* 51 (4): 23–27.

Chapter 7

Other Impacts of Natural Disasters

Media Framing, Crime, and Categorical Inequality

Timothy Holler and Reneè D. Lamphere

Given what we know about the trends in global disasters, particularly in the growing number of people being affected, it is important to examine the impact of those disasters on all facets of human behavior. Most of the social science research which examines natural disasters and criminality limit their studies to quantitative analysis of crime rates pre- and post-disaster. While this is important to understand the depth of impact that natural disasters can have, there is a minimal understanding of the effect that existing categorical inequality has on the criminal justice system post-disaster, or even how the post-disaster *perception* of criminality effects members of different categories. For example, can being a member of the lower class, or of a minority group, differentially impact the way institutions like the criminal justice system respond to the social and physical needs of effected citizens following a natural disaster?

Crime is a phenomenon that has proven to be both a cause and effect of social inequality. The apertures in the moral argument for a "just system" are clearly apparent in a society that executes the law differently based on one's socioeconomic status, racial category, or gender. The differential application of the law is so well known, in fact, that criminologists have actually dichotomized criminal behavior into crime committed by low-class, blue-collar individuals, and crime committed by high-class, white-collar individuals (Sutherland 1940, 1). This is similar to other socially defined dichotomies, or what Wood (2016) describes as "unequal paired categories" (30). Therefore, the dichotomization of criminality, both in social perception and legal execution, can be seen as extensions of the categorical inequality present in other paired categories such as race and socioeconomic status.

Defining crime in this manner also allows everyone, from policymakers to lay citizens, to quickly "understand" the nature of a criminal events, whether their understanding is accurate or not, and act upon their perception of the social importance of those events. From an institutional standpoint, this has created a system of unequal and inadequate responses to crime based on inaccurate perceptions of the social importance of criminal events. White-collar crime that costs individuals and companies billions of dollars a year, and can even cost people their lives, is seen as less socially important than interpersonal violence that effects a much smaller portion of the public (Michel 2016; Cohen 2014).

Discussing crime in a framework of accelerated categorical inequality such as this first requires the understanding that inequality is well-established and pre-existing (Wood 2016, 20). Second, it must be shown that the accelerant, in this case a natural disaster, in some way furthers the inequality among those pre-defined categories (Wood 2016, 20). Within this chapter, we argue that the phenomenon of accelerating categorical inequality happens, in places like New Orleans and Puerto Rico, because of the priority that is given to a constricted range of crime, while systematically ignoring the true nature of crime in these extreme circumstances. As will be shown, media focus and governmental responses, including those of the police, are situated on order maintenance in times of natural disaster. Squatting, drug sales, and looting become of primary concern, and less attention is paid to crimes of violence like rape and sexual assault as well as the crimes of white-collar criminals (Thornton and Voight 2010a, 2010b).

We further argue that the media's framing of events of great social importance has a devastating impact on the differential and inappropriate institutional responses to crime in the wake of natural disasters, particularly for those groups already marginalized and otherized by society. More specifically, we believe that disaster preparedness, and skewed political and social responses to disaster relief, are correlated with the dissemination of crime and disaster-related propaganda that disproportionately impact the poor. Using a comparative approach that looks at both historical and recent disaster events, we will examine both the empirical and perceived nature of crime and the impact this has on potentially accelerating categorical inequality.

The following chapter first outlines the media's role in framing existing categorical inequality and the institutional responses that are guided by those frames. We then examine the media's framing of criminality in the wake of the natural disasters that occurred in places like New Orleans and Puerto Rico. Next, we address post-disaster institutional decisions made regarding crime that reflect media biases rather than the true nature of crime. Finally, we address the potential affect this has on furthering categorical inequality and the need to research these phenomena further in order to adequately prepare more appropriate crime and disaster preparedness.

FRAMING CATEGORICAL INEQUALITY, CRIME, AND INSTITUTIONAL RESPONSES

It has become increasingly evident that the media, social or otherwise, is one of the most powerful institutions in the world. Because of its global reach and nearly inescapable boundaries, the media has enough power to influence everything from democratic elections to how we approach the minutia of seemingly innate human behavior. Applying this influence to how we perceive each other, both within and between groups, on categorical divisions such as poverty, race, and crime, provides a backdrop to the prevailing sentiment that is present in a post-disaster response framework.

While the idea of media framing in general refers to the way the media provides meaning to events, Surette (2015) more specifically describes a media frame as "a fully developed social construction template that allows its users to categorize, label, and deal with a wide range of world events. Frames simplify one's dealing with the world by organizing experiences and events into groups and guiding what are seen as the appropriate policies and actions" (38). The key concern of media framing is the simplification of extremely complex issues. This, often over-simplification, is what allows for the partitioning of acceptable social responses that fall within the range of the frame's explanatory power. This is often true of crime where frames allow us to compartmentalize, and therefore simplify things like criminal motive, investigations, and court room processes and outcomes.

For example, individuals who subscribe to, what Surette (2015) calls, the "Blocked Opportunities" frame can easily argue that "crime stems from poverty and inequality" and therefore it is the responsibility of the government to "create jobs and reduce poverty." What these frames also carry with them are symbolic types of crime, or social problems, that citizens can easily attach the frame to in order to inform their opinion on the potential policy solution for that issue. For instance, "black-on-black crime" and "dead-end, low-paying jobs" are emblematic within the blocked-opportunities framework (Surette 2015, 38).

Rose and Baumgartner (2013) examined the shifting role of public policy on poverty from 1960 to 2008. They based part of their research on the media's fluctuating interpretation on the causes of poverty, or rather how the media frames poverty and those whom are impoverished. What is clear from their research is that the media continues to play an increasing role in framing individual and institutional responses to existing inequality. The authors showed that shifting media discourse impacts the way society responds to those most in need. They note that current attention is situated squarely on the belief that "The poor are individually responsible for their problems, and that government efforts to help them may do more harm than good" (43).

This is an important distinction to make as it absolves social institutions of the responsibility to act, and furthermore sets the precedent for inaction in a post-disaster response framework.

The issues of race, crime, and poverty are not mutually exclusive. As debates on poverty often conjure images of blight and personal inaction, discussions on race and crime are inextricably linked to the vision of the "ghettoized" and often violent black predator. Specifically, images like those of Willie Horton, who all but sealed Michael Dukakis's fate in the 1988 presidential election often become engrained in our social consciousness (Welch 2007, 282). Thus, the link between blackness and crime is something woven into the very fabric of American culture. From slavery, black codes, and Jim Crow laws, to mass incarceration, African-Americans have always been portrayed as inherently violent and in need of corrective action (Gray and Cram 2017; Welch 2007, 282). As Welch (2007) suggests, "Because the media presumably have the power to help construct the meaning of race in our society, it is apparent that they play a significant role in defining Blacks as criminals as a result of the way they are often presented to readers and viewers" (283). Therefore, mediated perceptions of blackness that trigger racially motivated policing tactics like "Stop and Frisk" are what help to paint the perspective of inequity and its effects.

Much like current public policy regarding poverty reflects an antiquated social and political standpoint of "picking oneself up by the bootstraps," policy views on criminality currently harken back to the days of "Law Order" that typified the racially divisive "Southern Strategy" employed most notably by the Nixon administration, but by both Republicans and Democrats alike since (Zeitx 2016). Reactivity and corrective action come to define our formal policies regarding all three categories of poverty, race, and crime. Rather than take legislative action against the structures that keep people in poverty, or against disproportionate minority contact, we choose to police and criminalize the behavior of individuals who are in the midst of a traumatic event. It should come as no surprise then that typical media framing that is present pre-disaster, which aids in the systematic ignorance toward the needs of the nation's most disenfranchised, is both apparent and exacerbated following natural disasters.

FRAMING CATEGORICAL INEQUALITY AND INSTITUTIONAL "JUSTICE" POST-DISASTER

While the visible impact of natural disasters is apparent, with the number of disasters occurring each year, there is growing concern over the unseen damage that is inflicted (Thornton and Voight 2010a, 27; Toumayan 2010,

140). According to the Global Assessment Report on Disaster Risk Reduction (GAR) from 2015, financial losses globally from extreme climate events like earthquakes, tsunamis, cyclones, and flooding, are estimated at $314 billion annually (GAR 2015). Further, a 2016 report by the World Bank found that the annual impact of extreme disasters is $520 billion globally, and forces some 26 million individuals into poverty each year (World Bank 2016). The United States in 2018 "experienced the 4th highest total costs (91.0)" due to the 14 "billion-dollar disasters" (Smith 2019). We have also seen the number of billion-dollar events increasing with the past 5-year average (2014–2018) averaging 12.6 events, which is over double the 38-year average from 1980 to 2018 of 6.2 (Smith 2019).

The 2016 World Bank study of 117 counties showed losses from disasters disproportionately affected the poor, as these individual have less ability to cope when disaster strikes, pushing them further into poverty. In addition to financial costs, the estimated loss of human life internationally was 42 million human life years between 1980 and 2012 (GAR 2015, 7). With this increase in disasters, the number of people affected by these events is also increasing (Thornton and Voigt 2010a, 27). Poorer areas often suffer the greatest impact of natural disasters, facing a financing gap if they do not have the resources to buffer against disaster-related losses (Thornton and Voight 2010a, 27). Global issues such as climate change are only expected to exacerbate the amount of natural disasters in the future (GAR 2015, 8).

With the potential for disasters to increase exponentially with shifting climate, there is a need to understand how categorical inequality is framed following a disaster event and how this shapes institutional responses to that event. Two storms which provide perfect examples of how society responded socially and politically based on media framing are Hurricanes Katrina in 2005 and Maria in 2017. The fact that these storms are twelve years apart is beneficial because it shows that even when confronted with the notion of inadequate institutional responses, as we were following Hurricane Katrina, we made many of the same mistakes over a decade later after Hurricane Maria devastated the U.S. territory of Puerto Rico.

Both the categorical inequity which existed prior to, and was accelerated by, Hurricane Katrina has been well documented (Bolin 2007; Martin et al. 2016; Wood 2016). However, it is important to try and understand the role that media framing had on driving the discourse, both socially and institutionally, following the storm. In studying the intersectionality of disasters, media, race, crime, and poverty, Voorhees et al. (2007) show how disproportionate and inaccurate media framing were used to potentially influence, and in some case cover-up, inappropriate governmental responses to the widespread devastation while systematically disadvantaging those whom may have needed the most help following the storm.

To understand how a government, and more so an entire nation of people, can look at the same disaster event differently, one has to look no further than media framing. As Voorhees et al. (2007) address, "Two images of Hurricane Katrina survivors were paraded side by side as proof that the news media was biased against African-Americans—one image shows a black person carrying supplies labelled as 'looting,' while white people in an identical situation were labelled as 'finding' supplies" (416–417). With stories like this, and the dozens, if not hundreds of others that focused primarily on individualized criminality, we begin to gain a clearer picture of why institutional responses to the disaster focused primarily on keeping "Law and Order" (Berger 2007, 492).

What we saw following Hurricane Katrina then was not a well-thought-out, or even systematic approach, to dealing with disaster relief, but rather a haphazard, misinformed attempt at regaining institutional control over what the government saw as the "dangerous" black populous. We know now that most of the reports of random violence, looting, and criminal disorder were largely over-blown, and in many cases, patently false (Berger 2007, 492). Rather than expanding the efforts of rescuing people from their homes, and finding shelter for those who became displaced, these inaccurate reports are what drove institutional responses to the disaster (Voorhees et al. 2007). This is done through what Barnes et al. (2008) describe as agenda setting. "Agenda setting influences public agendas and policies through deliberate coverage of events and issues, with the media prompting policymakers to take action and satisfy the public's interest and demand for answers" (Barnes et al. 2008, 604).

Berger (2007) does an excellent job in explaining how disaster reporting during Katrina led to inappropriate relief efforts. He notes that "[the] construction of a looter class occurred amid a real environmental and human catastrophe, and its deployment curbed relief efforts." As is seen from much of the "normal" social policy that addresses, or fails to address, the nature of poverty and crime, officials decided to employ more officers and weaponry to focus on "eviction rather than evacuation" (501). The consequences of the misplaced relief efforts potentially increased the number of those, mostly poor individuals, who would parish in storm. These efforts also seemingly exacerbated the categorical inequality that existed in New Orleans, as institutions like the criminal justice system collapsed under the pressure of order-maintenance policing which left indigent misdemeanor offenders to "[languish] indefinitely in state prisons" (Murty and Hughley 2015, 1).

Sommers et al. (2006) address the misguided media coverage that existed following Hurricane Katrina, and the role that race played in shaping that media coverage and, in turn, societal attitudes toward victims of the storm. The authors examined the language used in describing victims, the angle of news stories, and the use of "new media" as a means of delivering accounts of the storm. They found that the term "refugee," which was briefly used immediately following the storm, as well as the media's increased focus on ultimately unsubstantiated violent criminality, may have impacted the public's perception of displaced persons, rendering them less worthy of the public's sympathy and support. It can be argued that those same perceptions of unworthiness are extended to policy makers who determine the course of disaster responses efforts. The use of refugee language in particular, is noted by the authors as being unique to Hurricane Katrina reporting, and as never being used before in describing U.S. citizens fleeing disaster. However, the same can now be said of Hurricane Maria survivors, as simple Google searches yield results as recent as September 2019 describing survivors of Hurricane Maria as "refugees."

While the research on Hurricane Maria is much less extensive, as it only occurred a little less than a year ago, media framing and political discourse are following many of the same patterns that were seen following Katrina. Puerto Rico prior to Hurricane Maria was not immune to the categorical inequality that exists in the contiguous United States, and in fact, is most likely more susceptible to inequity due to its total economic dependence on the United States or what Safa (2011) calls 'welfare colonialism' (48). To illustrate this inequality Todd (2014) states that "It is estimated that the poverty rate in Puerto Rico is 44.9 percent while the figure in Mississippi, the U.S. mainland's poorest state, is place at 24.2 percent." Poverty is not the only categorical inequity that exists in Puerto Rico, race also contributes to levels of discrimination and can be traced back to some of the same policies that disenfranchised blacks throughout history.

As Nixon touted his law and order policies to address poor, black criminality, there was one other group that Nixon also often addressed; Puerto Ricans. "Nixon recognized this connection when he privately reviewed one of his campaign's hard-hitting television ads in 1972 about urban crime and remarked, this 'hits it right on the nose. It's all about law and order and the damn Negro-Puerto Rican groups out there'" (Zeitz 2016). It again should come as no surprise then that headlines in the wake of disaster relief efforts following Hurricane Maria /focus on two consistent themes, total loss of power, and murder rates. Headlines such as "Puerto Rico fears post-Maria murder surge after 32 killed in 11 days" or "Puerto Rico Loses Power – Again" (AP 2018; Domonoske 2018).

These headlines play on many of the same racial and class-based tropes that illicit the immediate ire of readers and eliminate any "moral" justification for sending appropriate aid to "foreign countries" as "only 54 percent of Americans know that people born in Puerto Rico, a commonwealth of the

United States, are U.S. citizens" (Dropp and Nyhan 2017). Couple this with a collapse of the criminal justice system, particularly within police departments, and the situation in Puerto Rico only becomes even more ominous (Richards 2018). What is also different about the situation in Puerto Rico is that rather than sending the national guard and the military to impose a pseudo-martial law, the U.S. government, because of the lack of empathy by the U.S. people which was echoed by President Trump, were able to take a much more direct approach to ignoring the needs of these U.S. citizens (Reyes 2017).

WHAT IS IGNORED? LEGITIMATE CRIME CONCERNS POST-DISASTER

Crime committed during a natural disaster is of particular interest because it often represents a choice to escalate injury in the wake of already immeasurable suffering (Thornton and Voight 2010a, 29). Natural disasters cut across all groups of people, regardless of age, race, or socioeconomic status (Thornton and Voight 2010a, 29). However, much as how crime in general is not randomly distributed across social space and groups, research on disasters suggest that certain individuals, particularly the poor, are most affected by disasters (Thornton and Voight 2010a, 29; Toumayan 2010, 140). This includes loss of income, loss of households, loss of life, and loss of health (Thornton and Voight 2010a, 30). Certainly other risk factors are connected with crime during disasters, particularly victimization, such as race and ethnicity, gender, age, and disability; however, as will be shown, these variables are all arguably compounded by poverty (Thornton and Voight 2010a, 30).

In exploring why the poor may be disproportionately affected, Ferris (2010) argues that those who are poor are more likely to live in less safe environments, and after a disaster strikes, seek refuge in similarly less safe shelters. Areas with homes that are inadequately constructed are more vulnerable to earthquakes, landslides, and flooding and are often located in areas where the rich do not live (Ferris 2010). This was apparent during Hurricane Katrina in 2005, where the poorest areas of New Orleans, those south of Lake Pontchartrain, were the areas with the worst flooding (ABC News 2005). More than 700,000 people in that region lived in mobile homes, and many did not own a car and could not evacuate from harm's way. These individuals, mostly black, were sheltered in the Superdome, where they were vulnerable to increased victimization (ABC News 2005). While the research on crime and natural disasters has been limited in scope, there are studies that have assessed criminality following disasters. These studies give us an indication into what types of crime-related disaster relief policies we should be focusing on, including interpersonal violence and white-collar criminality.

NATURAL DISASTERS AND
INTERPERSONAL VIOLENCE

Research on crime relative to natural disasters demonstrates that interpersonal crimes have been observed in the wake of disaster. These crimes include murder, hate crimes, rape and sexual assault, child abuse, and domestic violence (Frailing 2016, 20). For example, Frailing discussed the increase in murder in New Orleans following Hurricane Katrina, some of which has been attributed to the reorganization of the drug market due to the storm (Frailing 2016, 20).

There is also reason to believe that child abuse may increase following a natural disaster. Curtis et al. (2000, 1151) examined child abuse rates following Hurricane Hugo and the Loma Prieta earthquake in 1989. It was found that child abuse reports were significantly higher in the 9-month time period following this disaster (Curtis et al. 2000, 1156). The most common type of child abuse reported in the wake of these disasters was physical abuse, which is in contrast to ordinary times when neglect is the most commonly reported type of abuse (Curtis et al. 2000, 1157). Examining this increase in physical abuse, according to the World Health Organization (WHO), in North Carolina following Hurricane Floyd in 1999, the rate of traumatic brain injury (TBI) to children under the age of two increased fivefold in the six-month period following the storm. This increase was seen in counties severely affected by the hurricane, as there was less or no increase in TBI in counties not affected (WHO 2005).

Before discussing the role of domestic violence during natural disasters, it is important to note that the number of empirical studies regarding domestic violence and disaster are scant (Thornton and Voigt 2010b, 110). The research that does exist demonstrates that domestic violence increases during natural disasters (Frailing 2016, 22; Khan 2016, 460). This increase is found in both descriptive studies (Clemens et al. 1999, 200; U.S. Department of Veteran's Affairs n.d.), and in proxy measures such as calls to the police and domestic violence hotlines, or reports to shelters (Jenkins and Phillips 2008, 50; Jenkins et al. 2016, 395; Phillips et al. 2010, 290). For example, following Hurricane Andrew in 1992, domestic violence calls to the community hotline in Miami, Florida increased by 50 percent (NCTSN 2014). As discussed by the National Child Traumatic-Stress Network (NCTSN), there are many factors that contribute to increases in domestic violence following natural disasters. An increase in domestic violence cases may be related to stressors that surround the disaster, such as loss of housing or employment. These losses may leave a perpetrator feeling an overall loss of control with life, and they may abuse their partner as a means of gaining control back in their personal relationships (NCTSN 2014). Further, those who were living in a violent relationship prior to a disaster may experience increased violence post-disaster as they may be separated from their support system of family and friends (WHO 2005).

The NCTSN (2014) gives several suggestions that can be used as part of disaster preparedness plans in terms of combating domestic violence. Prior to a disaster, a domestic violence focus should be included in interagency disaster response networks, and domestic violence shelters should be assisted in developing and reviewing their disaster plans (NCTSN 2014). During a disaster, a uniform and well-known protocol for domestic violence reporting and responding should be in place, with safe and secure shelter options being identified for victims and their children. Following a disaster, officials should continue to raise public awareness regarding domestic violence, and look to connect domestic violence and disaster survivors to long-term recovery resources (NCTSN 2014).

Another interpersonal crime that is often reported in the wake of disaster is rape and sexual assault (Frailing 2016, 23; Kahn 2016, 462; NSVRC 2008; Phillips et al. 2010, 292; Rozario 1997, 260; WHO 2005). Increased rates of sexual violence have been seen during times of natural disaster around the world. For example, during the Loma Prieta earthquake in California in 1989, reports of sexual violence increased by 300 percent (NSVRC 2008). Increased reports of sexual assault were also reported during Hurricane Katrina in 2005 (NSVRC 2008; Voigt and Thornton 2016, 150), the Boxing Day tsunami in 2004 (Teh 2008, 205), the South Asian tsunami of 2004 (NSVRC 2008), and the 2010 Haitian earthquake (Sloand et al. 2017, 3201), among others. Finding specific information on the rate of sexual violence following a disaster is difficult, especially given the limited empirical research on this topic, and even less so in the United States (Voigt and Thornton 2016, 150). As discussed by the NSVRC (2008), much like times without disaster, sexual violence that occurs during and after a disaster is often denied. In fact, following Hurricane Katrina, many media outlets issued reports that stories of sexual violence following the storm, particularly those accounts from those who sought refuge in the Super Dome, were "greatly exaggerated," and were rumors (NSVRC 2008). However, both official and unofficial reports of sexual violence provide evidence that sexual violence did occur in the time period during and after Hurricane Katrina (NSVCR 2008; Voigt and Thornton 2016, 150).

Two risk factors that often correlate with natural disasters and interpersonal victimization are sex and age. Women and children are particularly vulnerable to rape and sexual assault both during, and following, natural disasters (Frailing 2016, 23; Voigt and Thornton 2016, 151; WHO 2005). There are various reasons as to why women are at an increased risk of victimization in the wake of disaster. As discussed by Thornton and Voigt

(2010b, 111), women in natural disasters have special vulnerabilities, often including economic and racial disadvantages. Women in particular are more likely to have caregiver responsibilities, and these may leave them with an inability to evacuate during a disaster (Frailing 2016, 24). These women may subsequently be relocated to shelters or temporary housing, which often lack security (especially in economically deprived areas) leaving them vulnerable to predatory victimization (Frailing 2016, 24; Voigt and Thornton 2016, 151). Further, being in a shelter or in temporary housing may force a separation from family and friends, resulting in a lack of a communal support system (Voigt and Frailing 2016, 151). Another problem woman may experience is that there is nowhere to report a rape or sexual assault in a disaster-stricken area, especially when law enforcement is focused primarily on search and rescue (Frailing 2016, 24). Criminal behavior during natural disasters is certainly not limited to interpersonal violence; white-collar criminality has also become a widespread phenomenon (Davila et al. 2005, 272).

NATURAL DISASTERS AND WHITE-COLLAR CRIME

Another area of criminal victimization that is of interest to discuss in the context of natural disasters is white-collar offenses, particularly that of fraud. These are crimes which, by and large, do not necessitate a frame in order to understand them, because they are simply not reported on. The lack of media representation surrounding these crimes is indicative of the nature of media agenda setting through post crime reporting. Because white-collar criminality does not peak the interests of viewer's claims of rampant and random violent criminality come to define the post-disaster reporting structure which draws even more attention away from marginalized citizens who are being taken advantage of by white-collar offenders.

The term fraud in general is a complex and multidimensional term, used to describe everything from check fraud to identity theft (Davila et al. 2005, 272). Fraud and disaster can both be extremely costly. According to the National White Collar Crime Center [NW3C], fraud during disaster typically occurs through five primary strategies; fraudulent charitable solicitations, price gouging, contractor and vendor fraud, property insurance fraud, and forgery. The insurance industry estimates fraud losses at approximately 10 percent (NW3C 2017). Applying this 10 percent estimate to something like the Federal Emergency Management Agency (FEMA) Disaster Relief Fund, which at year end 2017 exceeded $73 billion in spending, the loss to disaster fraud could easily be $7.3 billion annually (NW3C 2017). This is money that would otherwise go toward providing relocation services and the rebuilding of infrastructure.

Contract fraud has become an increased concern as individuals and businesses are often reliant on the services of others. Before discussing contract fraud, it is again worth noting that the vulnerability of individuals trying to rebuild their lives only exacerbates this issue, especially those who are poor. FEMA (2018) released a study which found that low-income homeowners were not only disproportionately more likely to live in flood-prone areas, they were also less likely to purchase flood insurance. One could argue that those without insurance are especially susceptible to contract fraud, as they are working to rebuild their homes without monetary assistance. As defined by Davila et al. (2005) contractor fraud "typically involves an agreement between two parties where the first party pays the second for work that is never completed" (272). This also includes work that is completed, but is below the agreed upon standards, or overcharging for work (Davila et al. 2005, 273).

Contractor fraud was seen following Hurricane Marilyn in 1995 and Hurricane Fran in 1996 (Davila et al. 2005, 273). For example, after Hurricane Fran, a contractor in North Carolina submitted false claims and statements to FEMA regarding waterline repair projects, and was eventually sentenced to 15 months in federal prison and $45,000 in restitution (Davila et al. 2005, 274). The authors also studied the aftermath of the June 2001 flooding from Tropical Storm Allison in Harris County (Houston), Texas, and rain storm flooding in July 2002 in the mid-South Texas region. Surveying 1,000 residents per event, they found a total of 17 victims of contractor fraud. Most of the victims (13) were without any form of flood insurance, and the average estimated losses were $10,000. Davila et al. (2005) suggested that socially disorganized community conditions following a nature disaster may enhance opportunities for crime, even inviting fraudsters into the affected areas to prey on individuals in need (Davila et al. 2005, 289).

To help combat fraud during disaster, in September 2005 the Disaster Fraud Task Force was established to deter and detect fraud (NW3C 2017). The task force was created in direct response to Hurricane Katrina. The Task Force includes the Criminal Division, United States Attorneys' Offices, the FBI, the Postal Inspection Service, the U.S. Secret Service, the Federal Trade Commission, the Securities and Exchange Commission, Federal Inspectors General, and various representatives of state and local law enforcement (NW3C 2017). In addition to this, it was recognized that disaster-related fraud may disproportionately impact low-income residents, sparking the creation of Disaster Legal Services by FEMA. Disaster Legal Services is staffed by members of the American Bar Association Young Lawyers Division (ABA-LYD), and provides counsel and legal representation free of charge for low-income persons effected by a natural disaster (NW3C 2017). Further, in January 2008 President George Bush signed the Emergency and Disaster Assistance Fraud Penalty Enhancement Act into law, increasing penalties and sentences for fraudulent activity related to national disasters (NW3C 2017). While all of these services and laws are in place, it is unclear the effect they are having on disaster-related fraud, and more research is needed to study the impact of anti-fraud legislation.

DISCUSSION

When examining categorical inequality in a mediated world it is evident that the way we perceive those who occupy different categories from ourselves is colored by the media's interpretation and representation of those categories. This is true of poverty, race, and crime and can be furthered by natural disasters. Lack of governmental response to systematic racial and class biases in areas where disaster strikes tend to become conflated as governmental agencies mirror the media's uniformed and inaccurate reporting of crime. The inequality that existed in both New Orleans and Puerto Rico prior to these events, was manipulated and used by the media to further categorize survivors as undeserving, unappreciative of any relief efforts taking place, and more importantly, as violent criminals. Therefore, the categorical inequality that was present in these areas pre-disaster, which are a result of public policy models that encourage personal adherence to the law and the social contract rather than government intervention and accountability, allowed the government to take a post-disaster stance of either limiting crucial assistance, or of militarization and martial law.

With Hurricane Katrina, the categorization of survivors as refugees and criminals played on longstanding and well-established stereotypes that elicited a response of militarization and criminal prosecution. With Hurricane Maria, both President Trump and the media became responsible for establishing a narrative of Puerto Ricans as, at best, second-class citizens, but at worst, foreigners who were not worthy of governmental support. Therefore, it is important to recognize this manipulation of relief efforts by the media when developing disaster preparedness plans. Valuable resources including manpower and money, are wasted when allocated toward policing tactics such as "looter patrol." The government has a responsibility to provide for those in need no matter their race or socioeconomic status. Rather than criminalize the behavior of those suffering unimaginable trauma, we need to begin to the shift political and social discourse to more tangible and appropriate efforts of emergency management.

With the potential for natural disasters to increase it is evident that the social, political, and economic inequality that exists in areas at an increased risk of disaster needs to be addressed as a form of mitigation and prepared-ness. Beyond preparation, response and relief efforts need to be focused more heavily on those individuals already experiencing economic hardship. The media also needs to be held accountable for its role in generating and shifting public and political discourse around disasters and the relief efforts that fol-low. Finally, research should continue examining the extent through which disasters, natural or otherwise, can accelerate already existing categorical inequalities in certain areas. This should also include a comparative analysis of preparedness and response efforts that have occurred in more affluent areas of the country.

REFERENCES

ABC News. August 30, 2005. "Poorest Hit Hardest by Hurricane Katrina." Accessed June 22, 2018. https://abcnews.go.com/WNT/HurricaneKatrina/story?id=1081329 &page=1.

Associated Press. 2018. "Puerto Rico Fears Post-Maria Murder Surge After 32 Killed in 11 Days." *CBS News*, January 11, 2018. https://www.cbsnews.com/news/puerto -rico-fears-post-maria-murder-surge-after-32-killed-in-11-days/.

Barnes, Michael D., Carl L. Hanson, Len M. B. Novilla, Aaron T. Meacham, Emily McIntyre, and Brittany C. Erickson. 2008. "Analysis of Media Agenda Setting During and After Hurricane Katrina: Implications for Emergency Preparedness, Disaster Response, and Disaster Policy." *American Journal of Public Health* 98, no. 4: 604–610.

Berger, Dan. 2009. "Constructing Crime, Framing Disaster: Routines of Criminalization and Crisis in Hurricane Katrina." *Punishment and Society* 11, no. 4: 491–510.

Bolin, Bob. 2007. "Race, Class, Ethnicity, and Disaster Vulnerability." In *Handbook of Disaster Research*, edited by Havidàn Rodrìguez, Enrico L. Quarantelli, and Russell R. Dynes, 113–129. New York: Springer.

Clemens, Petra, Jennifer Hietala, Mamie J. Rytter, and Dona Reese. 1999. "Risk of Domestic Violence After Flood Impact: Effects of Social Support, Age, and History of Domestic Violence." *Applied Behavioral Science Review* 7: 199–208.

Cohen, Mark A. 2015. "Willingness to Pay to Reduce White-Collar and Corporate Crime." *Journal of Benefit-Cost Analysis* 6, no. 2: 305–324.

Curtis, Thom, Brent Miller, and E. Helen Berry. 2000. "Changes in Reports and Incidences of Child Abuse Following Natural Disasters." *Child Abuse & Neglect* 24, no. 9: 1151–1162.

Davila, Mario, James Marquart, and Janet Mullings. 2005. "Beyond Mother Nature: Contractor Fraud in the Wake of Natural Disasters." *Deviant Behavior* 26, no. 3: 271–293.

Domonoske, Camila. 2018. "Puerto Rico Losses Power—Again." *NPR*, April 18, 2018. https://www.npr.org/sections/thetwo-way/2018/04/18/603569966/puerto-rico-loses-power-again.

Dropp, Kyle, and Brendan Nyhan. 2017. "Nearly Half of Americans Don't Know Puerto Ricans Are Fellow Citizens." *The New York Times*, September 26, 2017. https://www.nytimes.com/2017/09/26/upshot/nearly-half-of-americans-dont-know-people-in-puerto-ricoans-are-fellow-citizens.html.

Federal Emergency Management Agency [FEMA]. April 17, 2018. "An Affordability Framework for the National Flood Insurance Program." U.S. Department of Homeland Security. Accessed June 22, 2018. https://www.fema.gov/media-library-data/1524056945852-e8db76c696cf3b7f6209e1adc4211af4/Affordability.pdf.

Ferris, Elizabeth. March 3, 2010. "Natural Disasters, Conflict, and Human Rights: Tracing the Connections." The Brookings Institute. Accessed June 22, 2018. https://www.brookings.edu/on-the-record/natural-disasters-conflict-and-human-rights-tracing-the-connections/.

Frailing, Kelly. 2016. "Toward a Criminology of Disaster." *ACJS Today* 41, no. 5: 19–28.

Global Assessment Report on Disaster Risk Reduction [GAR]. 2015. "GAR 2015 Main Report." Accessed June 18, 2018. https://www.preventionweb.net/english/hyogo/gar/2015/en/home/GAR_2015/GAR_2015_8.html.

Gray, Susan, and Bestor Cram dirs. 2017. *Independent Lens.* Season 18, "Birth of a Movement." Aired February 6, 2017, on PBS. http://www.pbs.org/independent lens/films/birth-of-a-movement/#.

Jenkins, Pamela, Bethany Van Brown, and Kimberly Mosby. 2016. "Rebuilding and Reframing: Non-Profit Organizations Respond to Hurricane Katrina." In *Crime and Criminal Justice in Disaster*, 3rd ed., edited by Dee Wood Harper and Kelly Frailing, 393–412. Durham: Carolina Academic Press.

Jenkins, Pamela, and Brenda Phillips. 2008. "Battered Women, Catastrophe, and the Context of Safety After Hurricane Katrina." *NWSA Journal* 20, no. 3: 49–68.

Khan, H. E. Nazhat. 2016. "Sexual and Gender-Based Violence in Natural Disasters: Emerging Norms." *Commonwealth Law Bulletin* 42, no. 3: 460–468.

Martin, Lori Latrice, Kenneth J. Fasching-Varner, and Melinda Jackson. 2016. "A Tale of Two Cities: Race and Wealth Inequality in the New South." In *After the Storm: Militarization, Occupation, and Segregation in Post-Katrina America*, edited by Lori Latrice Martin Hayward Derrick Horton, and Kenneth J. Fasching-Varner, 1–18. Santa Barbara: Praeger.

Michel, Cedric. 2016. "Violent Street Crime Versus Harmful White-Collar Crime: A Comparison of Perceived Seriousness and Punitiveness." *Critical Criminology* 24: 127–143.

Murty, Komanduri S., and Ronald Hughley. 2015. "Crime and Justice: Remorse, Redemption & Recovery After Katrina." *Race, Gender, & Class Supplement*: 283–302.

National Child Traumatic-Stress Network [NCTSN]. 2014. "Disasters and Domestic Violence: A Factsheet for Disaster Responders and Providers." Accessed June 18, 2018. http://dcc.missouri.edu/doc/dcc_domestic_violence_and_disasters.pdf.

National Sexual Violence Resource Center [NSVRC]. 2008. "Sexual Violence in Disasters: A Planning Guide for Prevention and Response." Accessed June 18, 2018. https://www.nsvrc.org/publications/nsvrc-publications/sexual-violence-disasters-planning-guide-prevention-and-response.

National White Collar Crime Center [NW3C]. June 2017. "Disaster Fraud." Accessed June 18, 2018. https://www.nw3c.org/docs/research/disaster-fraud.pdf.

Peek, Lori, and Michelle Meyer. 2016. "When Hate Is a Crime: Temporal and Geographic Patterns of Anti-Islamic Hate Crime After 9/11." In *Crime and Criminal Justice in Disaster*, 3rd ed., edited by Dee Wood Harper and Kelly Frailing, 247–270. Durham: Carolina Academic Press.

Phillips, Brenda, Pam Jenkins, and Elaine Enarson. 2010. "Violence and Disaster Vulnerability." In *Social Vulnerability to Disasters*, edited by Brenda Phillips, Deborah Thomas, Alice Fothergill, and Lynn Blinn-Pike, 279–303. Boca Raton, FL: CRC Press.

Reyes, Raul A. 2017. "Trump's Lack of Empathy About Puerto Rico Is Staggering." *CNN*, September 26, 2017. https://www.cnn.com/2017/09/26/opinions/trumps-lack-of-empathy-about-puerto-rico-reyes/index.html.

Rose, Max, and Frank R. Baumgartner. 2013. "Framing the Poor: Media Coverage and U.S. Poverty Policy, 1960–2008." *The Policy Studies Journal* 41, no. 1 (February): 22–53.

Rozario, Santi. 1997. "Disasters and Bangladeshi Women." In *Gender and Catastrophe*, edited by Ronit Lenten, 255–268. New York: Zed Books.

Safa, Helen. 2011. "The Transformation of Puerto Rico: The Impact of Modernization Ideology." *Transforming Anthropology* 19, no. 1: 46–49.

Sloand, Elizabeth, Cheryl Killion, Hossein Yarandi, Phyllis Sharps, Annie Lewis-O'Connor, Mona Hassan, Faye Gary, Nicole Muller Cesar, and Doris Campbell. 2017. "Experiences of Violence and Abuse Among Internally Displaced Adolescent Girls Following a Natural Disaster." *Journal of Advanced Nursing* 73, no. 12: 3200–3208.

Smith, Adam B. 2019. "2018's Billion Dollar Disasters in Context." National Oceanic and Atmospheric Administration. Accessed November 30, 2019. https://www.climate.gov/news-features/blogs/beyond-data/2018s-billion-dollar-disasters-context.

Sommers, Samuel R., Evan P. Apfelbaum, Kristin N. Dukes, Negin Toosi, and Elsie J. Wang. 2006. "Race and Media Coverage of Hurricane Katrina: Analysis, Implications, and Future Research Questions." *Analyses of Social Issues and Public Policy* 6, no. 1: 1–17.

Surette, Ray. 2015. *Media, Crime, and Criminal Justice: Images, Realities, and Policies*. Stamford: Cengage Learning.

Sutherland, Edwin. 1940. "White-Collar Criminality." *American Sociological Review* 5, no. 1 (February): 1–12.

Teh, Koon Yik. 2008. "The Abuses and Offenses Committed During the Tsunami Crisis." *Asian Criminology* 3, no. 2 (December): 201–211.

Thornton, William, and Lydia Voigt. 2010a. "Disaster Phase Analysis and Crime Facilitation Patterns." In *Crime and Criminal Justice in Disaster*, edited by Dee Wood Harper and Kelly Frailing, 27–59. Durham: Carolina Academic Press.

Thornton, William, and Lydia Voigt. 2010b. "Disaster Rape: Vulnerability of Women to Sexual Assaults during Hurricane Katrina." In *Crime and Criminal Justice in Disaster*, edited by Dee Wood Harper and Kelly Frailing, 107–138. Durham: Carolina Academic Press.

Todd, Jack. 2014. "Poverty in Puerto Rico." *Borgen Magazine*, March 14, 2014. http://www.borgenmagazine.com/poverty-puerto-rico/.

Toumayan, Meredith. 2010. "Are Natural Disasters Increasing?" *School Library Journal* 56, no. 11: 140.

U.S. Department of Veteran's Affairs. n.d. "Disasters and Domestic Violence: Prevalence and Impact of Domestic Violence in the Wake of Disasters." June 18, 2018. Accessed June 7, 2018. https://www.ptsd.va.gov/professional/trauma/disaster-terrorism/disasters-domestic-violence.asp.

Voigt, Lydia, and William Thornton. 2016. "Disaster-Related Rape and Sexual Assaults in Pre-and-Post Hurricane Katrina." In *Crime and Criminal Justice in Disaster*, 3rd ed., edited by Dee Wood Harper and Kelly Frailing, 147–189. Durham: Carolina Academic Press.

Voorhes, Courte C. W., John Vick, and Douglas D. Perkins. 2007. "'Came Hell and High Water': The Intersection of Hurricane Katrina, the News Media, Race and Poverty." *Journal of Community & Applied Social Psychology* 17: 417–429.

Welch, Kelly. 2007. "Black Criminal Stereotypes and Racial Profiling." *Journal of Contemporary Criminal Justice* 23, no. 3 (August): 276–288.

Wood, Geoff. 2016. "Accelerated Categorical Inequality: New Orleans in the Eye of the Storm." In *After the Storm: Militarization, Occupation, and Segregation in Post-Katrina America*, edited by Lori Latrice Martin, Hayward Derrick Horton, and Kenneth J. Fashing-Varner, 19–32. Santa Barbara: Praeger.

World Bank. 2016. "Natural Disasters Force 26 Million People into Poverty and Cost $520bn in Losses Every Year, World Bank Analysis Finds." Accessed June 22, 2018. http://www.worldbank.org/en/news/press-release/2016/11/14/natural-disasters-force-26-million-people-into-poverty-and-cost-520bn-in-losses-every-year-new-world-bank-analysis-finds.

World Health Organization [WHO]. 2005. "Violence and Disasters." Accessed June 18, 2018. http://www.who.int/violence_injury_prevention/publications/violence/violence_disasters.pdf.

Zetix, Josh. 2016. "How Trump Is Recycling Nixon's 'Law and Order' Playbook." *Politico*, July 18, 2016. https://www.politico.com/magazine/story/2016/07/donald-trump-law-and-order-richard-nixon-crime-race-214066.

Chapter 8

The Way Forward—How Do We Improve Outcomes and Create Solutions for People Impacted by Natural Disasters?

Paul S. Adams and Geoffrey L. Wood

As we reflect back on the writings in this edited volume, there are numerous connections and recommendations made by scholars, from several disciplines including criminal justice, political science, and sociology, relevant to examining the impact of natural disasters on social inequality. This volume demonstrates that scholarly investigation of natural disasters and their social, economic, and political impacts are not restricted to one field or discipline. The inquiry into how natural disasters exacerbate and magnify social and economic inequalities finds traction in a wide range of social sciences including sociology, political science, criminology, economics, geography, public policy, and law. Although these authors approach the topic from differing perspectives, they all agree that this is a frequently overlooked but increasingly important topic in many fields. With the increasing incidence of natural disasters and their concussive effects upon those that have been socially, economically, and politically marginalized, the need for robust scholarly and theoretical frameworks to understand, explain, and potentially address such phenomena is in high demand. This concluding section will tie together these connections and recommendations in order to discover how we improve outcomes and create solutions for people impacted by natural disasters.

In the opening chapter of this volume, Wood introduces categorical inequality and critical demography as powerful tools to examine the lens through which social inequality shapes events during and following natural disasters. Rather than relying on individual status attainment measures of social inequality, Wood argues as scholars we should move toward models that allow for the measurement of power in a social system, rather than ones which rely on race, gender, and income alone. Instead of looking at individuals in terms of specific deficits as the reason for not doing well during a natural disaster, the focus should be shifted toward institutional, systemic, and structural factors which created and set in movement underlying social inequality. In an historically relevant approach, criminogenic, economic, political, social inequities are set in place before a natural disaster. Interestingly, authors in this volume showed across a variety of settings that natural disasters serve as an accelerant of already existing social inequality. The importance of models which allow for the inclusion of both history and power relations tend to provide stronger explanations for institutional and structural constraints than do individualized ones. For example, the institutionalization of categorical uneven pairs sets in social inequality in place from the beginning, and then adaptation and emulation allow institutions and organizations to duplicate existing unequal power relation already in place.

Consistent with theoretical strengths of categorical inequality and critical demography approaches, authors in ths volume make contributions toward solutions for people living through natural disaster or emergency events. Specifically, Loebach and Stewart conclude linking capital and vertical social ties are more important for outcomes of social inequality after a natural disaster than one's individual position alone. Rather than simply looking at individuals, how people are connected to others both before and after a disaster event is key to the sorts of resources from which they can draw. In their writing, structural measures are important ways to discover how individuals use social capital during a crisis.

When looking at election parameters and practices, Adams examines the hyper-decentralized processes of voting in America. He argues convincingly that natural disasters accelerate already uneven processes of democracy. Decentralization as well as the lack of unifying standards across jurisdictions allow for local entities to set, implement, and manage voting parameters which are often influenced by local power demographics as opposed to written rules and regulations. By allowing local jurisdictions to develop policies and procedures with little oversight and hyper-decentralization, elections and voting processes differ substantially across the United States. When a natural disaster or emergency event strikes, decentralized practices contribute to already high levels of social inequality across local areas. In places where social inequality by race, class, and gender is institutionalized and structured by existing power relationships, decentralized voting processes result in higher levels of social inequality as existing local power forces use the lack of standardized processes to their benefit. Adams argues that natural disasters tend to exacerbate these processes as local forces often become even more decentralized. Ultimately, the highly decentralized institutions of the American voting system are the critical variable.

Barreto contends that the bipolar nature of American citizenship plays a critical role in shaping the outcomes for people following a natural disaster. Specifically, he argues the way in which the Trump Administration treated Puerto Rico in the aftermath of Hurricane Maria supports the divided understandings and considerations of American citizenship. Barreto contends that ethnicity is a defining variable in terms of both institutions and structures in the case of Puerto Rico. Puerto Ricans, in fact U.S. citizens, were treated unequally and as second-class citizens on the bases of their racialized citizenship status coupled with race and the lack of power resulting in a lower socially structured position. In his extensive case study, Barreto concludes that Puerto Rico's racialized and perceived "foreign" status as a less than deserving colony by the Trump Administration shows a continuing pattern of deserving versus undeserving Americans in a natural disaster or crisis.

Rather than looking at the racialized nature of citizens directly, Prohaska examines class and race differences on perceptions of reconstruction and rebuilding following a tornado in Alabama. She finds that there are very different perceptions of the process and outcomes of community rebuilding and reconstruction that tend to vary by class and race. Local citizens of black, brown, or white of lower socioeconomic status reported often that the rebuilding process was less favorable and less inclusive of their interests and needs. Prohaska argues that these distinctions are not ones from individual decisions, but rather that the existing social inequality system was in face structuring the perceptions of the local residents. The perception by minority and economically disadvantaged citizen that their voice, demands, and needs were marginalized by the existing institutions responsible for recovery. Although Prohaska's work is local and qualitative in nature, she finds the importance of reified institutional and structural patterns of inequality consistent with other works in this volume.

Shifting to the criminal justice system as the area of analysis and investigation, Koch and Feaster discuss the ways in which the criminal justice functions and responds for offenders during natural disasters. They argue there are substantial institutional and structural barriers which prevent offenders from using reentry and disaster services during an emergency event. Koch and Feaster contend these barriers have long since been in place, but the natural disaster event allows local communities to fall back on systems and processes which hinder the ability of offenders to cope well through a disaster. They contend natural disasters tend to accelerate the barriers and existing trends toward offender, particularly intellectual disabled or sexual offenders. Once again, this correlates well with this volume's overarching theme of the lasting and critical impact of institutions and their replicated practices.

The work of Holler and Lamphere has a decidedly criminal justice focus more broadly analyzing post-disaster perceptions and the media framing of events entrenched in stereotypes and racism. Using Wood's work on historically developed categorical inequality as a starting point, Holler and Lamphere contend these categories become institutionalized into existing structures, which then leads to the ability of institutions and organizations to use these categories to structure social inequality. They argue that post-disaster perceptions of victims are often framed by the media along reified racist stereotypes. While white residents are reported as "searching for supplies," black residents of the same area are described as "looting" by local and national media. Holler and Lamphere further contend that this reliance on existing stereotypes allows media to shape the perceptions of the public that strongly resonate with preconceived notions of crime in America. Once the stereotypes are embedded, it is then quite easy for media to use these to frame and disseminate a message, which can then sharpen the edge of social inequality in communities as residents are viewed as deserving or undeserving on the basis of race. Holler and Lamphere conclude that once racialized media framing of residents is in place, existing stereotypes for the oversimplification of the disaster situation and already existent social inequality allow the media to reinforce categorical inequality following a natural disaster.

Following an examination of the chapters and topics of this volume, it is important to discover and discuss some potential solutions for the American people who have or will experience a natural disaster event. The incidence of natural disasters is increasing. With this growing incidence, the repercussions will not only also grow in incidents, but also in magnitude and in variety. Natural disasters by their very nature stress and magnify the operational patterns and codes of existing formal and informal social, economic, and political institutions. As an area of scholarly and policy inquiry and study, the demand for social scientists and policymakers to understand, explain, and respond to the challenges of natural disasters by possessing a fundamental understanding of how critical institutions are to exacerbating and magnifying existing inequalities. In this section, we will elaborate on some of the potential remedies to the impact of natural disasters on social inequality in the United States. First, rather than relying on individual analysis of residents in terms of demographics or income, a thorough examination of institutions and structures as well as the existing social inequality in place before natural disasters should be the starting point of analysis. Institutions and structures not only matter, they are the critical variable in understanding how inequality is made a routine and embedded element of the American society. Next, instead of starting from a color-blind, class-blind, or race-blind position, which assumes all residents have the same access to resources and power, the importance of history and ideology are key to understanding how and why systems of inequities are in place. The interaction of history and ideology is crucial and frequently reproduced through stereotypes by American media and information outlets. American media tends to highlight personal characteristics based on stereotypes of race, class, and gender, and the intersection of these that reinforces perceptions of deserving and undeserving citizens. This is amplified during a natural disaster or other major emergency. This simplified media framed typology places perceived less-deserving people at an institutional and structural disadvantage vis-à-vis more deserving ones.

In addition to the roles of mainstream media and social media in exacerbating social inequality during a natural disaster, there are numerous other targets. A serious look at neighborhood gentrification, the development and institutionalization of racism and racist structures, the haphazard governmental response at multiple fragmented and uncoordinated levels with the media serving to define, reify, and frame the contexts of those deserving help are areas where future research on this topic should concentrate. Rather than examine these measurements in individualized ways, scholars and researchers instead must look at institutionalized power structures to ascertain how this limits the decisions of those in lower positions of power. Power is a key element, but it is often overlooked in individual level analysis.

Finally, as a nation, we must move away from the current policies of the Trump Administration and similar such policies and rhetoric from state and local levels that seek to divide Americans by race, class, gender, and voting preferences into groups of deserving and undeserving citizens and residents. As was the case in Hurricane Maria in Puerto Rico, we cannot continue to allow for the creation of a status of undeserving Americans attached to those in less powerful and less structurally sound positions within the American social stratification system. A move away from Trumpian policies seeking to divide Americans on the basis of race, class, gender, citizenship, or some other undeserving status assigned and rebroadcast through our institutions and social and corporate media outlets. Rather than allowing outside actors to define and implement solutions to local problems, allowing the better integration of local residents, not just by race, class, or power, but instead by giving all an equal voice in discussions of how to move forward after a natural disaster. Social inequality has a long and painful relationship with a racist and discriminatory history, and these malignancies are salient themes of the American story. Rather than ignoring these, the most advantageous way forward is to address these systematically and in a forthright manner. By addressing the institutional and structural pieces of American society that are the sources and replicators of categorical inequality and discrimination, we can work to improve such conditions as well as lessen the impact of natural disasters.

Index

About the Editors and Contributors

Paul S. Adams, PhD, is an associate professor of Political Science and chair of the Behavioral Sciences Division at the University of Pittsburgh at Greensburg. His areas of academic research and teaching include Comparative Politics with an emphasis on election systems, federalism, political economy, corporatism, and consociationalism as well as studies of European politics including Ireland, Northern Ireland, Switzerland, the European Union, and Germany. He earned a PhD in Political Science from the University of Massachusetts-Amherst, an MA in International Affairs from Florida State University, and a BA in International Studies from George Mason University.

Geoffrey L. Wood, PhD, is an associate professor of Sociology and director of the Center for Applied Research at the University of Pittsburgh at Greensburg. His areas of academic research and teaching include categorical inequality, critical demography, diversity and race studies, and changes in social inequality over time. He earned a PhD in Sociology from the University at Albany–SUNY, a MA in Sociology from Sacramento State, and a BA in Sociology from Fresno State.

* * *

Amílcar Antonio Barreto, JD, PhD, is professor and interim chair in the Department of Cultures, Societies and Global Studies at Northeastern University in Boston. His research focuses on nationalism, ethnicity, race, and identity politics in Puerto Rico and Latino communities on the U.S. mainland. He is the author and coeditor of several books, including *The Politics of Language in Puerto Rico Revisited* (2020), *American Identity in* *the Age of Obama* (2014), *Nationalism and Its Logical Foundations* (2009), and *Vieques, the Navy, and Puerto Rican Politics* (2002).

Dennis Feaster is an associate professor of Social Work at Hope College. He received his Bachelors in Sociology and Law & Society from Purdue University in 1991, and a MSW from Indiana University (IUPUI) in 2000. He completed his PhD in Social Work in 2012, and focuses his research on issues related to disability and community in the United States and China.

Timothy J. Holler, PhD, associate professor of Criminal Justice at Pitt-Greensnburg, earned his BA, MA, and PhD in Criminology at Indiana University of Pennsylvania. His research areas predominantly include restorative justice, correctional programming, reintegration, and crime and media. Dr. Holler is a faculty affiliate for the Center for Applied Research and the director of the Community Arts and Reintegration Project. Dr. Holler also currently serves on the Westmoreland County CJAB, the Westmoreland County Reentry Committee, and the Pennsylvania Reentry Council. He is also an active member of the Academy of Criminal Justice Sciences where he serves as the vice-chair to the Restorative and Community Justice Section.

Pamela Ray Koch is an associate professor of sociology and the director of the peace studies minor at Hope College. She holds a master's in public administration from the University of Nebraska-Omaha and a PhD in sociology from the University of South Carolina. Her research focuses on public policy and social institutions and also the relationship between family and education.

Reneè D. Lamphere, PhD, is an associate professor of Criminal Justice in the Department of Sociology & Criminal Justice at the University of North Carolina at Pembroke. Her areas of academic interest include corrections, mixed-methods research, sexual violence and victimization, family violence, and cyber and digital-media crimes. Dr. Lamphere has a particular interest in teaching and pedagogy, and has published in the *Journal of Criminal Justice Education,* and does research on teachers and their role in K–12 school violence.

Pete Loebach is a faculty member at Arapahoe Community College, where he is program chair for the emergency services administration program. His areas of expertise include individual and community vulnerability, demographics of disasters and the national incident management system. His work on the topics of disasters and mass emergencies has been published in leading social science journals including *Social Science Review, Disasters, and Population and Environment.*

Ariane Prohaska is an associate professor of Sociology in the Department of Criminology and Criminal Justice at the University of Alabama. Her research interests include gender, bodies, fat studies, and disaster sociology. She has recently published in *Fat Studies, Critical Policy Studies,* and *International Journal of Mass Emergencies and Disasters.*

Julie Stewart, associate professor of Honors at Westminster College, holds a PhD in sociology from New York University. Her research examines the natural and unnatural forces behind displacement, how migrants create community, and why contexts of reception vary across communities, states and nations.